I0796255

ESSENTIALS
COCKTAILS

COCKTAILS

OVER 500 CLASSIC RECIPES

CONTENTS

INTRODUCTION

Compared to the oldest alcoholic beverages, which some researchers believe to have originated around 10,000 BCE, the cocktail is a relative newcomer to the spirits world, having been around for just a few hundred years—the first written record of the word "cocktail" occurs in *The Farmers Cabinet*, which was published in 1803.

Why, you might be wondering, did it take so long for the cocktail to emerge?

The answer depends on who you ask, but one powerful theory centers around the arrival of Prohibition in America—and it boils down to the reality that most of the alcohol available to the public was, to be frank, bad. Awful. Pure swill. Bootleggers needed a metaphorical spoonful of sugar to help their medicine go down, and the cocktail proved to be a godsend. Mixed drinks had been around for some time before the start of Prohibition, but once it arrived, they became all the rage. And as drinkers gathered in speakeasies and greedily imbibed these concoctions that made the rotgut they were used to seem refreshing, a social culture started to grow up around them.

Still, serving as a tentpole of social life is a long way off from evolving into an art form. But, over the last 25 or so years, that is precisely what happened—and a quick survey of the drinks scene today reveals the power of this unlikely development. All of a sudden, you can find a clarified milk punch in a sleepy mountain town. In chain restaurants, which thrive by shooting for the dead center of the road, carefully constructed drinks featuring mezcal, amaro, and house-made herbal syrups are routine, so commonplace that we don't even raise an eyebrow when we encounter them.

This book seeks to celebrate all of the cocktails that have become classics during this period. Some you may be able to make with the bottles you already have on hand. Others will encourage you to search out an ingredient whose existence you were previously unaware of. Still more will inspire you to reach for the top shelf, rather than trawling the lower levels looking for a bargain to add to your liquor cabinet.

You'll find plenty of touchstones that are built around familiar spirits, such as the Bloody Mary, Martini, Margarita, and Old Fashioned. But you'll also find drinks that feature far more exotic elements, such as aquavit, Chartreuse, and shochu. You'll find recipes that date back to the 1800s and startlingly modern concoctions. You'll find frozen cocktails, shooters, and drinks topped with luscious foam. You'll find spicy drinks, sweet drinks, and everything in between.

But, most importantly, you'll find drinks that are certain to expand your horizons and step up your cocktail game.

BASIC TECHNIQUES

DRY SHAKE

When a recipe asks you to "dry shake," that means to combine all of the drink's ingredients in a cocktail shaker without ice and shake. The dry shake is often used to emulsify drinks that include an egg white.

WHIP SHAKE

This involves rapidly shaking a cocktail shaker or mixing tin back and forth with both hands while keeping a tight grip on it, using a minimal amount of ice. This creates a frothy texture and adds considerably more air bubbles to the drink.

DOUBLE STRAIN

Eager to eliminate those pesky ice shards that end up in a drink? That's where the double strain comes in. It involves straining the drink twice—once through a regular strainer (i.e., a Hawthorne strainer) and then again through a fine-mesh strainer. This ensures that any ice shards or small pieces of fruit, herbs, or spices are caught and do not end up in the final cocktail.

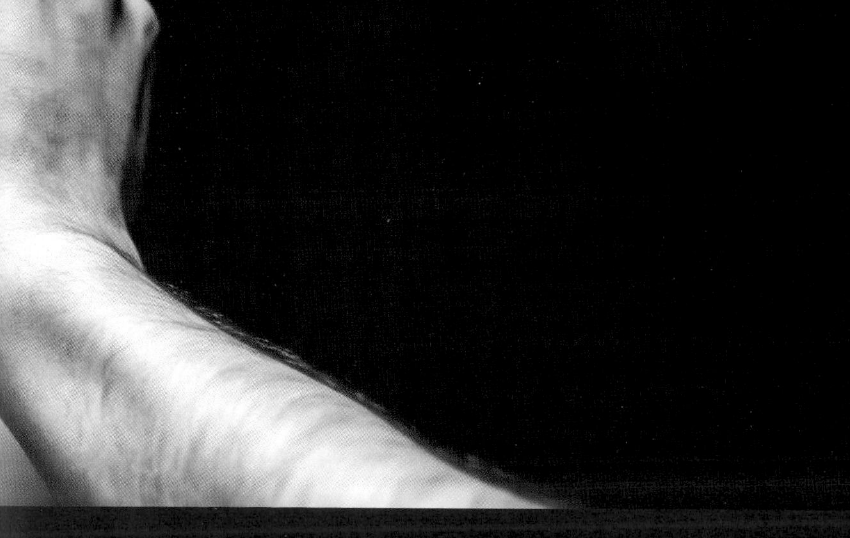

CUBAN ROLL

Residing in the space between shaking and stirring (more dilution and aeration than the latter and yet gentler than shaking), this method consists of pouring the ingredients and ice between two containers until they are chilled and combined.

SWIZZLE METHOD

Used to combine cocktails featuring crushed ice, the swizzle method will quickly chill and aerate the cocktail. Some bartenders believe that this method also further draws out the aromas of the drink's ingredients. To employ the swizzle method, fill a glass with crushed ice, strain the cocktail over it, and place a swizzle stick between your hands. Lower the swizzle stick into the drink, and quickly rub your palms together to rotate the stick as you move it up and down in the drink. When frost begins to form on the outside of the glass, the drink is ready.

RIMMING A GLASS

To proper rim a glass with salt, sugar, or spices, fill a small bowl with ¼ cup water and a shallow bowl with ¼ cup of whatever you are applying to the rim. Wet the rim of the glass in the water, roll the rim of the glass in the salt, sugar, or spices, ensuring an even coating, and gently shake off any excess.

ESSENTIAL TOOLS & GLASSWARE

There are not many things that you need to purchase in order to start crafting cocktails, but there are some rudimentary supplies that are necessary if you want to try your hand at this game.

The following pages contain the must-haves for a basic bar setup. Keep in mind that you don't have to break the bank to start your home bar, but between glassware and bar tools, a little money will need to be spent. You can find basic bar and glassware sets on specialty sites like Cocktail Kingdom, as well as at other online retailers. As with anything, the options will fit lots of budgets. If you are tight on funds, don't be deterred by secondhand items. Soap and water come pretty cheap and you might find some real bargains on vintage gear to boot. Same goes for antique shops and yard sales. Hell, your parents might have some of the tools you need stashed away in a closet or the basement. Nothing wrong with a little scavenging for a good cause.

JIGGER

"Jigger" is just a fancy name for the most common measuring tool in a bartender's arsenal, allowing you to quickly and easily measure ounces or "parts." Most have a similar shape and capacity to a shot glass.

MIXING GLASS

Nothing more than a tall glass in which to stir a drink. Typically a pint glass is used, but in a pinch, you can use any glass large enough to hold the necessary ingredients along with a few ice cubes.

COCKTAIL SHAKER

A cocktail shaker is a container about the size of a pint glass, usually made from metal, with a screw top. The shaker provides a simple way to mix a cocktail, combining the necessary ingredients, chilling them with ice, and diluting the cocktail slightly to remove the bite of the included spirits and allow their flavors to come to the fore. A basic cocktail shaker is relatively inexpensive, and you are better off purchasing this specific tool than trying to jury-rig a shaker for yourself.

The three-piece shaker, which is what you'll find in most homes, is known as the "Cobbler shaker." There are also two-piece shakers, consisting of two conical containers with flat bottoms, with one of the cones larger than the other. Known as a "Boston" or "French" shaker, these tend to be favored by professional bartenders because their "throw," the amount of space inside for the ingredients and ice to become combined, is greater than in the squatter Cobbler shaker.

HAWTHORNE STRAINER

Used in tandem with either a mixing glass or Boston shaker, the Hawthorne strainer simply strains the cocktail after it has been mixed. The strainer's spring keeps the ice cubes (in the case of a mixing glass) or broken ice chips (in the case of a Boston shaker) out of a drink. Because ice waters down a drink when it melts, the strainer is an important tool for keeping a cocktail pure.

You may also come across a Julep strainer as you start making your way into the world of mixology. This strainer, which was the predecessor to the Hawthorne, is a perforated, concave disk with holes in it. It has fallen out of common use, but is the preferred tool of some bartenders when straining a cocktail containing small pieces of herb or a large amount of pulp.

PARING KNIFE

Chances are, there's already one in your kitchen, and it is essential for crafting the lemon twists and lime wedges that are a crucial part of numerous cocktails.

MUDDLER

Similar to a pestle, this simple tool is used to mash ("muddle") ingredients such as fruits or herbs. Muddling fruits releases the juice within, adding a fresh characteristic to a drink, while muddling certain herbs helps activate their flavors. A simple muddler can often be found on the top end of a Cobbler shaker, though more refined muddlers are available for minimal cost.

BAR SPOON

There are plenty of fancy bar spoons, but most take the form of a spoon with a small bowl and a long, threaded shaft. Used in conjunction with a mixing glass, the purpose of the bar spoon is to quickly and easily stir any cocktail.

You can use any spoon—you just may find it more difficult to navigate the ice cubes. You will also come across some recipes that call for a "bar spoon" of a certain ingredient, which is equivalent to 1 teaspoon.

BOTTLES FOR HOMEMADE BITTERS & INFUSIONS

Making your own bitters and infusing liquors with herbs and spices are tremendous, and simple, ways to lift your bartending game to another level. A large mason jar also fits the bill.

COCKTAIL GLASSES

The elegant promise of the iconic thin stem and triangular bowl has become inseparable from the very idea of a cocktail, as evidenced by its frequent inclusion on a bar's signage. It is typically utilized in cocktails that are served "up," such as the Martini.

COLLINS & HIGHBALL GLASSES

Collins glasses are tall and skinny, and most commonly used in drinks that contain ice and a carbonated element such as club soda. Highball glasses are generally a little wider and shorter than Collins glasses, though the differences between them are so minimal that the two can be used interchangeably.

ROCKS GLASSES

Also known as Old Fashioned glasses, these are meant for neat drinks and spirits on the rocks. They are between 8 and 10 ounces; double rocks glasses are typically only a couple ounces larger and used for cocktails served over ice.

COUPES

The coupe has started to replace the traditional cocktail glass as the go-to for drinks that are served up, as its sleek curves lend a drink an appealing refinement.

SHOT GLASSES

There is no standard size for a shot glass, but most land between 1¼ and 1½ ounces. They can be used to measure parts for a cocktail or to serve alcohol, both straight up and mixed.

WINEGLASSES & CHAMPAGNE FLUTES

Both are sophisticated and celebratory. Wineglasses are wonderful for aromatic cocktails, while the thin bowl and delicate stem of a Champagne flute is a must for any sparkling cocktail.

VODKA

Vodka's lack of a distinctive flavor allows it to find a comfortable place beside a stunning amount of other ingredients, making it a perfect spirit for cocktails. You can pair it with damn near anything, as evidenced by its presence in a diverse group of cocktails that spans from Martinis to Bloody Marys and White Russians. It plays well with many other spirits and complements whatever it is added to, which is not something you can say about other types of alcohol. This ease puts many cocktail aficionados off, but in the cocktail world, every hardline stance is simply the progenitor of considerable opportunities. And, as you'll soon see, a number of leading bartenders and mixologists have seized upon them, filling the substantial open space with unusual ingredients and innovative blends that will delight vodka enthusiasts, and win over those who are skeptical of the spirit.

MILANO

1½ oz. Effen Blood Orange Vodka
¾ oz. Aperol
1 oz. fresh lemon juice
½ oz. Simple Syrup (see recipe)
½ oz. egg white
1 oz. Prosecco, plus more to top

Chill a Champagne flute in the freezer.

Place all of the ingredients, except for the Prosecco, in a cocktail shaker containing 1 large ice cube and shake until chilled.

Pour the Prosecco into the chilled Champagne flute and strain the cocktail over it.

Top with additional Prosecco and enjoy.

Simple Syrup: Place 1 cup sugar and 1 cup water in a saucepan and bring to a boil, stirring to dissolve the sugar. Remove the pan from heat and let the syrup cool completely before using or storing.

PERESTROIKA

1 lime wedge
Dash of caster (superfine) sugar
2 slices of English cucumber, plus 1 for garnish
2 oz. vodka
½ oz. pear nectar

Place the lime wedge and sugar in a cocktail shaker and muddle.

Add ice and the remaining ingredients, except for the garnish, and shake until chilled.

Strain into a coupe, garnish with the additional slice of cucumber, and enjoy.

MILANO

CLASSIC ESPRESSO MARTINI

CLASSIC ESPRESSO MARTINI

2 oz. vodka

1 oz. freshly brewed espresso

½ oz. coffee liqueur

3 espresso beans, for garnish

Chill a cocktail glass in the freezer.

Place the vodka, espresso, and liqueur in a cocktail shaker, fill it two-thirds of the way with ice, and shake until chilled.

Double strain into the chilled cocktail glass and garnish with the espresso beans.

ETRENNE

½ oz. vodka

⅔ oz. green banana liqueur

2 bar spoons mint liqueur

½ oz. heavy cream

1 green cocktail cherry, for garnish

Place all of the ingredients, except for the garnish, in a cocktail shaker, fill it two-thirds of the way with ice, and shake vigorously until chilled.

Double strain into a cocktail glass, garnish with the green cocktail cherry, and enjoy.

DUNBAR'S NUMBER

½ oz. fresh citrus
7/10 oz. lychee liqueur
7/10 oz. blanc vermouth
1 oz. vodka
1½ oz. bitter orange liqueur
4 oz. iced hibiscus tea
1 oz. sparkling sake

Place all of the ingredients, except for the sparkling sake, in a cocktail shaker, fill it two-thirds of the way with ice, and shake until chilled.

Add the sparkling sake, strain the cocktail over 1 large ice cube into a tumbler, and enjoy.

COPPER CUP

2 oz. Absolut Elyx Vodka
¾ oz. St-Germain
¼ oz. freshly pressed ginger juice
¾ oz. fresh lemon juice
¼ oz. Hibiscus Syrup (see recipe)
1 slice of fresh ginger, for garnish
1 orchid blossom, for garnish

Place all of the ingredients, except for the garnishes, in a cocktail shaker, fill it two-thirds of the way with ice, and shake vigorously until chilled.

Fill a copper cup with crushed ice, strain the cocktail over it, and top with more crushed ice.

Garnish with the slice of ginger and orchid blossom and enjoy.

Hibiscus Syrup: Place 1 teaspoon loose-leaf hibiscus tea in 1 cup Simple Syrup (see page 16) and steep for 10 days. Strain before using or storing in the refrigerator.

GINGER BINGER

1½ oz. vodka
Splash of triple sec
1½ oz. grapefruit juice
3 oz. ginger ale
1 lime wheel, for garnish
1 sprig of fresh mint, for garnish

Fill a highball glass with ice, add the vodka, triple sec, and grapefruit juice, and stir until chilled.

Top with the ginger ale and gently stir to combine.

Garnish with the lime wheel and fresh mint and enjoy.

LEMON DROP

Sugar, for the rim
2 oz. vodka
1 oz. triple sec
1 oz. fresh lemon juice
1 lemon twist, for garnish

Wet the rim of a cocktail glass and rim it with sugar.

Place the vodka, triple sec, and lemon juice in a cocktail shaker, fill it two-thirds of the way with ice, and shake until chilled.

Strain into the rimmed cocktail glass, garnish with the lemon twist, and enjoy.

LEAVE IT TO ME

2 oz. Grey Goose Vodka

¼ oz. Lazzaroni Maraschino liqueur

¾ oz. Raspberry Syrup (see recipe)

¾ oz. fresh lemon juice

1 oz. egg white

3 raspberries, for garnish

Place all of the ingredients, except for the garnish, in a cocktail shaker and dry shake for 15 seconds.

Add ice and shake until chilled.

Double strain the cocktail into a coupe, garnish with the raspberries, and enjoy.

Raspberry Syrup: Combine 1 lb. raspberries and 1 lb. sugar in a deep saucepan, then gently press down the mixture with the back of a fork. Let it macerate for 15 minutes, then add 2 cups water. Bring the mixture to just below a boil. Remove the pan from heat and let the syrup cool for 30 minutes. Strain the syrup through a fine-mesh sieve or cheesecloth before using or storing in the refrigerator.

ARCTIC WARMER

4 oz. hot tea

Unsalted butter, to taste

2 oz. vodka

1 oz. tequila

Dash of cinnamon

1 to 2 cinnamon sticks, for garnish

Place the tea and butter in a mug and stir until the butter melts.

Add the vodka, tequila, and cinnamon and stir until thoroughly combined.

Garnish with 1 or 2 cinnamon sticks and enjoy.

LEAVE IT TO ME

WHITE RUSSIAN

As everyone knows, the Coen Brothers' late '90s masterwork, *The Big Lebowski*, breathed considerable life into this creamy cocktail, which had lost its way during the calorie-conscious 1980s. By bringing this easy and delicious crowd-pleaser back into vogue, they just may have bought their unorthodox film—and the reluctant sage at the center of it—some of the considerable cachet they now carry.

While "The Dude" is laid back enough to tolerate powdered creamer and generic half-and-half in his "Caucasian," it pays to be a bit more discerning about the dairy component—no matter how big a fan of the movie you are. As you want a White Russian to feel as indulgent and rich as possible, heavy cream, with its minimum fat content of 36 percent, is essential. If heavy cream's thickness makes you wary, add just enough to lighten the drink slightly. Should you or a guest be one of those individuals who can't get enough coffee flavor, consider filling your ice-cube trays with room-temperature coffee for cubes that will bolster the taste and prevent your drink from becoming too watery. Also, take your time composing this one, as the sight of the heavy cream purling in the glass is sure to set tongues wagging.

1½ oz. vodka
½ oz. Kahlúa
Heavy cream, to top

Fill a rocks glass with ice, add the vodka and Kahlúa, and top with heavy cream.

Gently stir until chilled and enjoy.

CAPE COD

1½ oz. vodka
5 oz. cranberry juice
1 lime wedge, for garnish

Chill a highball glass in the freezer.

Fill the glass with ice, add the vodka and cranberry juice, and stir until chilled.

Garnish with the lime wedge and enjoy.

GREYHOUND

1 oz. vodka
Grapefruit juice, to top

Fill a highball glass with ice, add the vodka, and top with grapefruit juice.

Stir until chilled and enjoy.

VODKA GIMLET

1½ oz. vodka
½ oz. fresh lime juice
1 lime wedge, for garnish

Place the vodka and lime juice in a mixing glass, fill it two-thirds of the way with ice, and stir until chilled.

Strain into a cocktail glass, garnish with the lime wedge, and enjoy.

SEX ON THE BEACH

½ oz. vodka

1 oz. peach schnapps

2 oz. orange juice

2 oz. cranberry juice

Fill a Collins glass with ice, add the vodka and peach schnapps, and top with the orange juice and cranberry juice.

Stir until chilled and enjoy.

SCREWDRIVER

1 oz. vodka

Orange juice, to top

Fill a highball glass with ice, add the vodka, and top with orange juice.

Stir until chilled and enjoy.

MIND ERASER

¾ oz. coffee liqueur

¾ oz. vodka

¾ oz. tonic water

Layer the coffee liqueur, vodka, and tonic water in a double shot glass by pouring them over the back of a spoon and enjoy.

BERRIES & BUBBLES

BERRIES & BUBBLES

3 to 4 fresh raspberries

1½ oz. vodka

½ oz. Simple Syrup (see page 16)

½ oz. fresh lemon juice

1½ oz. Champagne or sparkling rosé

1 edible flower blossom, for garnish

Chill a coupe in the freezer.

Place all of the ingredients, except for the Champagne and garnish, in a cocktail shaker, fill it two-thirds of the way with ice, and shake until chilled.

Double strain the cocktail into the chilled coupe.

Top with the Champagne, garnish with the edible flower blossom, and enjoy.

HARVEY WALLBANGER

1 oz. vodka

4 oz. fresh orange juice

¼ oz. Galliano

1 orange slice, for garnish

Fill a Collins glass with ice, add the vodka and orange juice, and top with the Galliano.

Stir until chilled, garnish with the orange slice, and enjoy.

POMEGRANATE COSMO

1½ oz. vodka

½ oz. PAMA Pomegranate Liqueur

½ oz. Pierre Ferrand Dry Curaçao

½ oz. fresh lime juice

½ oz. pomegranate juice

Place all of the ingredients in a cocktail shaker, fill it two-thirds of the way with ice, and shake until chilled.

Strain into a cocktail glass and enjoy.

THE TWELFTH NIGHT

1 oz. Absolut Citron

½ oz. triple sec

½ oz. white cranberry juice

Splash of fresh lime juice

Splash of lemon-lime soda

Fresh mint, for garnish

Place the vodka, triple sec, and white cranberry juice in a cocktail shaker, fill it two-thirds of the way with crushed ice, and shake until chilled.

Strain over ice into a rocks glass and top with the lime juice and soda.

Garnish with fresh mint and enjoy.

POMEGRANATE COSMO

ITALIAN GREYHOUND

CLASSIC VODKA MARTINI

2 oz. vodka
½ oz. dry vermouth
1 lemon twist, for garnish

Place the vodka and vermouth in a mixing glass, fill it two-thirds of the way with ice, and stir until chilled.

Strain into a cocktail glass, garnish with the lemon twist, and enjoy.

ITALIAN GREYHOUND

1 oz. vodka
½ oz. Cappelletti
½ oz. St. George Spirits Bruto Americano
Fresh grapefruit juice, to top
1 grapefruit wheel, for garnish

Place a giant ice cube in a rocks glass. Add the vodka, Cappelletti, and Bruto Americano, top with grapefruit juice, and stir until chilled.

Garnish with the grapefruit wheel and enjoy.

THE DIRTY SPY

3 oz. vodka
1 oz. dry vermouth
Splash of green olive brine
Pimento-stuffed green olives, for garnish

Place the vodka, vermouth, and olive brine in a cocktail shaker, fill it two-thirds of the way with ice, and shake until chilled.

Strain into a cocktail glass, garnish with olives, and enjoy.

THE PICKLE KID

2 oz. vodka

1 oz. pickle brine

1 slice of pickle, for garnish

Chill a cocktail glass in the freezer.

Place the vodka and pickle brine in a mixing glass, fill it two-thirds of the way with ice, and stir until chilled.

Strain into the chilled cocktail glass, garnish with the pickle, and enjoy.

HAIRY NAVEL

1½ oz. vodka

1½ oz. peach schnapps

4 oz. orange juice

Splash of pineapple juice

1 orange slice, for garnish

Fill a mason jar with ice, add the vodka and peach schnapps, and top with the orange juice and pineapple juice.

Stir until chilled, garnish with the orange slice, and enjoy.

ANGEL'S KISS

1 oz. chocolate vodka

1 oz. skim milk

3 drops of grenadine

Place a large ice cube in a rocks glass, add the chocolate vodka, and then float the skim milk on top, pouring it slowly over the back of a spoon.

Add the grenadine, let it filter down through the cocktail, and enjoy.

BLUE LAGOON

2 oz. vodka

1 oz. blue curaçao

2 oz. fresh lemon juice

2 oz. club soda

1 lemon slice, for garnish

Fill a mason jar with ice, add the vodka, blue curaçao, and lemon juice, and top with the club soda.

Stir until chilled, garnish with the lemon slice, and enjoy.

APPLETINI

1½ oz. vodka

½ oz. Sour Apple Pucker

½ oz. triple sec

3 apple slices, for garnish

Place the vodka, Sour Apple Pucker, and triple sec in a cocktail shaker, fill it two-thirds of the way with ice, and shake until chilled.

Strain into a cocktail glass, skewer the apple slices on a cocktail pick, garnish the cocktail with them, and enjoy.

THE SLAMMER

1 oz. vodka

1 oz. amaretto

1 oz. Southern Comfort

3 oz. orange juice

Fill a highball glass with ice, add the vodka, amaretto, Southern Comfort, and orange juice, stir until chilled, and enjoy.

BLUE HAWAIIAN

¾ oz. vodka
¾ oz. Pusser's Rum
½ oz. blue curaçao
3 oz. pineapple juice
1 oz. Sweet & Sour (see recipe)
½ cup ice
1 dehydrated pineapple slice, for garnish
Pineapple leaves, for garnish

Place all of the ingredients, except for the garnishes, in a blender and puree until smooth.

Pour the cocktail into a Hurricane glass, garnish with the dehydrated pineapple slice and pineapple leaves, and enjoy.

Sweet & Sour: Place 2 oz. fresh lemon juice, 4 oz. fresh lime juice, and 6 oz. Demerara Syrup (see page 65) in a mason jar, seal it, and shake until combined. Use immediately or store in the refrigerator.

CRANBERRY LEMONADE

Sugar, for the rim
½ oz. vodka
½ oz. fresh lemon juice
½ oz. cranberry juice

Wet the rim of a shot glass and rim it with sugar.

Place the vodka, lemon juice, and cranberry juice in a cocktail shaker, fill it two-thirds of the way with ice, and shake until chilled.

Strain into the rimmed shot glass and enjoy.

BLUE HAWAIIAN

MOSCOW MULE

MOSCOW MULE

Juice of ½ lime

2 oz. vodka

6 oz. ginger beer

1 lime wedge, for garnish

1 sprig of fresh mint, for garnish

Fill a copper mug with crushed ice, add the lime juice and vodka, and top with the ginger beer.

Stir until chilled, garnish with the lime wedge and fresh mint, and enjoy.

ONE BIG HOLIDAY

Sugar, for the rim

4 oz. pear juice

2 oz. vanilla vodka

Drop of almond extract

1 pear slice, for garnish

Wet the rim of a mason jar and rim it with sugar.

Place the pear juice, vodka, and almond extract in a cocktail shaker, fill it two-thirds of the way with ice, and shake until chilled.

Strain into the rimmed mason jar, garnish with the pear slice, and enjoy.

ELEVATED ESPRESSO MARTINI

¾ oz. vodka

1 oz. cold-brew coffee

1 oz. Mr Black Coffee Liqueur

¼ oz. sweetened condensed milk

3 espresso beans, for garnish

Place all of the ingredients, except for the garnish, in a cocktail shaker, fill it two-thirds of the way with ice, and shake until chilled.

Double strain into a Nick & Nora glass, garnish with the espresso beans, and enjoy.

MUDSLIDE

1 oz. vodka

1 oz. coffee liqueur

1 oz. Irish cream

1 oz. heavy cream

Dash of chocolate syrup

1 cup ice

Dollop of whipped cream

1 sprig of fresh mint, for garnish

Place the vodka, coffee liqueur, Irish cream, heavy cream, chocolate syrup, and ice in a blender and puree until smooth.

Pour the cocktail into a Hurricane glass or mason jar and top with the whipped cream.

Garnish with the fresh mint and enjoy.

ELEVATED ESPRESSO MARTINI

OCEAN BREEZE

1 oz. vodka

1 oz. gin

1 oz. grapefruit juice

3 oz. cranberry juice

1 oz. Sprite

Place the vodka, gin, grapefruit juice, and cranberry juice in a highball glass and stir to combine.

Add ice and stir until chilled.

Top with the Sprite, gently stir to combine, and enjoy.

SAPPORO

1 oz. vodka

2 bar spoons amaretto

2 bar spoons Green Chartreuse

2 bar spoons dry vermouth

1 green cocktail cherry, for garnish

Place all of the ingredients, except for the garnish, in a mixing glass, fill it two-thirds of the way with ice, and stir until chilled.

Strain into a cocktail glass, garnish with the green cocktail cherry, and enjoy.

SEA BREEZE

1½ oz. vodka
¼ oz. fresh lime juice
3 oz. cranberry juice
1½ oz. grapefruit juice
1 grapefruit slice, for garnish
1 cherry, for garnish

Fill a highball glass with ice, add the vodka, lime juice, cranberry juice, and grapefruit juice, and stir until chilled.

Garnish with the grapefruit slice and cherry and enjoy.

CREAMSICLE

1 oz. orange juice
1 oz. vodka
1 oz. heavy cream
Splash of triple sec
1 orange slice, for garnish

Place the orange juice, vodka, cream, and triple sec in a cocktail shaker, fill it two-thirds of the way with ice, and shake until chilled.

Strain over ice into a rocks glass, garnish with the orange slice, and enjoy.

SEA BREEZE

COSMOPOLITAN

COSMOPOLITAN

2 oz. Grey Goose Vodka

1 oz. triple sec

1 oz. cranberry juice

½ oz. fresh lime juice

1 lime wheel, for garnish

Place the vodka, triple sec, cranberry juice, and lime juice in a cocktail shaker, fill it two-thirds of the way with ice, and shake until chilled.

Strain into a cocktail glass, garnish with the lime wheel, and enjoy.

PEACH TREE ICED TEA

6 fresh mint leaves, torn in half

1 oz. peach schnapps

1 oz. vodka

2 oz. iced tea

Place the mint leaves and peach schnapps in a rocks glass and muddle.

Add the vodka, iced tea, and ice to the rocks glass, stir until chilled, and enjoy.

BLOODY MARY

As those who have mastered this particular recipe are all too aware, this cocktail is too good to be restricted to brunch, where its glory can easily be clouded by long waits and mediocre, overpriced egg dishes. Refreshing, invigorating, and able to facilitate any number of innovations, it's just a matter of time before this becomes a go-to morning, noon, and night.

While this recipe rightly states that you should garnish your Bloody Mary with whatever you bloody like, we would like to make a plea for the inclusion of the most recognizable of its numerous garnishes—the celery stalk—for those who are turning to it as a hangover remedy. Celery has a long history as a curative, with its medicinal use noted as far back as *The Odyssey*. Knowing that it has long been used to treat colds, the flu, digestive ailments, and issues with water retention, it makes perfect sense that someone looking to take the edge off their hangover with a Bloody Mary would add a celery stalk as an additional restorative.

4 dashes of kosher salt
2 dashes of cayenne pepper
2 dashes of ground black pepper
6 dashes of Worcestershire sauce
½ oz. fresh lemon juice
2 oz. vodka
2 oz. tomato juice

Fill a pint glass with ice, add all of the ingredients, and stir until chilled.

Garnish with whatever your heart desires and enjoy.

YUZU & MATCHA MARTINI

YUZU & MATCHA MARTINI

1½ oz. vodka
1 oz. fresh grapefruit juice
1 bar spoon yuzu juice
1 bar spoon matcha powder
1 strip of grilled yuzu peel, for garnish

Place all of the ingredients, except for the garnish, in a cocktail shaker, fill it two-thirds of the way with ice, and shake until chilled.

Strain into a cocktail glass, garnish with the strip of grilled yuzu peel, and enjoy.

WINTER VITAMIN

1¾ oz. vodka
2 teaspoons Cynar
2 teaspoons Aperol
2 teaspoons honey
2 teaspoons lime juice
2 bar spoons apricot jam
1¾ oz. freshly pressed carrot-apple juice
2 dashes of celery bitters

Place all of the ingredients in a cocktail shaker, fill it two-thirds of the way with ice, and shake until chilled.

Strain into a rocks glass and enjoy.

EQUISSE NO. 1

1¾ oz. Grey Goose Pear Vodka
1½ oz. white grape juice
4 teaspoons fresh grapefruit juice
4 teaspoons fresh lime juice
¾ oz. Vanilla Syrup (see recipe)

Place all of the ingredients in a cocktail shaker, fill it two-thirds of the way with ice, and shake until chilled.

Strain into a coupe and enjoy.

Vanilla Syrup: Place 1 cup water in a small saucepan and bring it to a boil. Add 2 cups sugar and stir until it has dissolved. Remove the pan from heat. Halve 1 vanilla bean and scrape the seeds into the syrup. Cut the vanilla bean pod into thirds and add the pieces to the syrup. Stir to combine, cover the pan, and let the mixture sit at room temperature for 12 hours. Strain the syrup through cheesecloth before using or storing.

EAST OF EDEN

1½ oz. vodka
½ oz. coconut rum
¼ oz. heavy cream
½ oz. egg white
½ oz. fresh lemon juice
½ oz. Simple Syrup (see page 16)
2 dashes of lavender bitters

Place all of the ingredients in a cocktail shaker, fill it two-thirds of the way with ice, and shake until chilled.

Strain into a coupe and enjoy.

EAST OF EDEN

ZIGGY STARDUST

MR. FUNK

1 oz. peach vodka

1 oz. cranberry juice

Sparkling wine, to top

1 lemon twist, for garnish

Fill a rocks glass with ice, add the vodka and cranberry juice, and top with sparkling wine.

Gently stir until chilled, garnish with the lemon twist, and enjoy.

ZIGGY STARDUST

1¾ oz. Lemon-Infused Vodka (see recipe)

2 teaspoons crème de cassis

1¾ oz. pomegranate juice

½ oz. fresh lemon juice

1 egg white

Edible pink glitter, for garnish

Place all of the ingredients, except for the garnish, in a cocktail shaker and dry shake for 15 seconds.

Add ice and shake until chilled.

Strain into a cocktail glass, garnish with edible pink glitter, in the shape of the iconic *Aladdin Sane* lightning bolt, and enjoy.

Lemon-Infused Vodka: Peel 1 lemon, place the peel in a mason jar filled with vodka (or directly in the bottle of vodka), and steep for 24 to 36 hours. Strain before using or storing.

CHILTON

Salt, for the rim
1½ oz. vodka
Juice of 2 lemons
Topo Chico, to top
1 lemon wheel, for garnish

Wet the rim of a highball glass and rim it with salt.

Fill the rimmed glass with ice, add the vodka and lemon juice, and top with Topo Chico.

Stir until chilled, garnish with the lemon wheel, and enjoy.

BERRIES FROM THE WEST

2 oz. blueberry vodka
1 oz. Simple Syrup (see page 16)
1 oz. fresh lemon juice
1 lemon wheel, for garnish
Blueberries, for garnish

Place the vodka, syrup, and lemon juice in a cocktail shaker, fill it two-thirds of the way with ice, and shake until chilled.

Strain over ice into a rocks glass, garnish with the lemon wheel and blueberries, and enjoy.

ZEITOUNI

4 fresh basil leaves

2 teaspoons Simple Syrup (see page 16)

1 fresh pineapple slice

3 Granny Smith apple slices

2 oz. Ketel One Citroen Vodka

1 teaspoon extra-virgin olive oil

Pinch of kosher salt

Pinch of black pepper

Chill a coupe in the freezer.

Place the fresh basil and syrup in a cocktail shaker and muddle. Add the pineapple and apple and muddle until they release their juices.

Add the vodka, olive oil, salt, and pepper to the shaker, fill it two-thirds of the way with ice, and shake until chilled.

Strain into the chilled coupe and enjoy.

AMELIA

1½ oz. vodka

1 oz. Blackberry Puree (see recipe)

¾ oz. St-Germain

½ oz. fresh lemon juice

Fresh mint, for garnish

Chill a coupe in the freezer.

Place the vodka, Blackberry Puree, St-Germain, and lemon juice in a cocktail shaker, fill it two-thirds of the way with ice, and shake until chilled.

Place some mint in your palm and smack it with your other hand to release the aroma.

Strain the cocktail into the chilled coupe, garnish with the mint, and enjoy.

Blackberry Puree: Place ¼ lb. fresh or thawed frozen blackberries, 2 tablespoons caster (superfine) sugar, 2 tablespoons water, and 2 tablespoons fresh lemon juice in a blender and puree until smooth. Strain before using or storing.

GIN

When working with gin to make a cocktail, you want to use its powerful, herbal, and woodsy nature to your advantage. You don't want to try and hide it, as it will take too much effort, and likely leave you with a drink that tastes clumsy, inarticulate. Instead, you want to highlight its character as best you can, either surrounding it with floral, herbal, and vegetal elements, setting it off with fruity and spicy elements, or leaning upon gin's most reliable partners—citrus, vermouth, and bitters. Gin's strong flavor forces you to keep an important rule in cocktail making front of mind—it is always best to err on the side of simplicity with your creations. You'll see some exceptions to that approach here, as rules were made to be broken. But you will not see any cocktails where gin's strong backbone is saddled with too much to carry.

AVIATION

2 oz. gin

½ oz. Luxardo maraschino liqueur

¼ oz. crème de violette

½ oz. fresh lemon juice

1 Luxardo maraschino cherry, for garnish

Chill a cocktail glass in the freezer.

Place the gin, Luxardo, crème de violette, and lemon juice in a cocktail shaker, fill it two-thirds of the way with ice, and shake until chilled.

Strain into the chilled cocktail glass, garnish with the maraschino cherry, and enjoy.

BLOOD ORANGE COCKTAIL

1½ oz. gin

⅓ oz. Amaro Averna

1 oz. fresh blood orange juice

Chill a cocktail glass in the freezer.

Place the gin, amaro, and blood orange juice in a cocktail shaker, fill it two-thirds of the way with ice, and shake until chilled.

Strain into the chilled cocktail glass and enjoy.

WHITE WINE MARTINI

2 oz. gin

1 oz. white wine

3 grapes, for garnish

Place the gin and white wine in a mixing glass, fill it two-thirds of the way with ice, and stir until chilled.

Strain into a cocktail glass, skewer the grapes on a toothpick, garnish the cocktail with them, and enjoy.

ANNE WITH AN E

2 oz. London dry gin

¾ oz. fresh lemon juice

½ oz. curaçao

½ oz. Honey Syrup (see recipe)

¾ oz. egg white

2 drops of 10 Percent Saline Solution (see recipe)

1 large strip of grapefruit peel

Green Chartreuse, to spritz

1 edible flower petal, for garnish

Chill a coupe in the freezer.

Place all of the ingredients, except for the Green Chartreuse and garnish, in a cocktail shaker and dry shake for 15 seconds.

Add ice and shake until chilled.

Double strain the cocktail into the chilled coupe, spritz it with Green Chartreuse, garnish with the edible flower petal, and enjoy.

Honey Syrup: Place 1½ cups water in a saucepan and bring it to a boil. Add 1½ cups honey and cook until it is just runny. Remove the pan from heat and let the syrup cool before using or storing in the refrigerator.

10 Percent Saline Solution: Place 1 oz. salt in a measuring cup. Add warm water until you reach 10 oz. and the salt has dissolved. Let the solution cool before using or storing.

SCORPION BOWL

2 oz. fresh lime juice

4 oz. fresh orange juice

1 oz. Demerara Syrup (see recipe)

2 oz. Orgeat (see page 103)

1 oz. grenadine

2 oz. brandy

4 oz. London dry gin

4 oz. rum

1 Flaming Lime Shell (see recipe), for garnish

Place all of the ingredients, except for the garnish, in a cocktail shaker and pour it into another cocktail shaker or mixing glass to combine.

Divide the cocktail between two large vessels, add crushed ice to each, and flash mix with a hand blender.

Pour the contents of the vessels into four goblets or a ceramic Scorpion bowl, garnish with the Flaming Lime Shell, and enjoy.

Demerara Syrup: Place 1 cup water in a saucepan and bring it to a boil. Add ½ cup demerara sugar and 1½ cups sugar and stir until they have dissolved. Remove the pan from heat and let the syrup cool completely before using or storing.

Flaming Lime Shell: Squeeze the juice out of a lime half and then fill it with 151-proof rum. Set it atop the cocktail. Using a long match, light the rum on fire and sprinkle cinnamon over the flame to make it spark. Enjoy the show and wait until the flame burns out to enjoy the drink.

MARTINI

A cocktail that has weathered every shift in fashion and managed to retain its place as the epitome of refinement. A drink that, working with just two ingredients, is able to astound seasoned aficionados and dazzle the uninitiated. Easy to make and difficult to master, revered for its simplicity and adaptability, the Martini is a cocktail one could spend a life with, as noted by American historian Bernard DeVoto, who once said, "It is one of the happiest marriages on earth, and one of the shortest lived."

While much discussion has centered around decoding the secrets behind a perfect Martini, the true key is, fittingly, pretty simple: work with a quality vermouth. It is a small, and frequently maligned, part of the Martini, but assuming this is an indication that it is unimportant will take you far afield. Once you incorporate this lesson, the Martini is an exercise in restraint. It can be tempting to add more gin to the mix, or to toss the ingredients into a shaker since cold seems to be key, but it is imperative that you take your cue from the drink itself, and refrain from messing around.

4 oz. London dry gin
1 oz. dry vermouth
1 lemon twist, for garnish

Chill a cocktail glass in the freezer.

Place the gin and vermouth in a mixing glass, fill it two-thirds of the way with ice, and stir until chilled.

Strain into the chilled cocktail glass, garnish with the lemon twist, and enjoy.

THE ELDER FASHION

2 oz. Plymouth Gin
½ oz. St-Germain
Dash of orange bitters
1 grapefruit twist, for garnish

Place the gin, St-Germain, and orange bitters in a mixing glass, fill it two-thirds of the way with ice, and stir until chilled.

Strain the cocktail over ice into a rocks glass, garnish with the grapefruit twist, and enjoy.

DIXIE COCKTAIL

1 oz. gin
1 oz. fresh orange juice
1 tablespoon sambuca
½ oz. dry vermouth

Chill a cocktail glass in the freezer.

Place the gin, orange juice, sambuca, and vermouth in a cocktail shaker, fill it two-thirds of the way with ice, and shake until chilled.

Strain into the chilled cocktail glass and enjoy.

GIN SOUR

2 oz. gin
1 oz. fresh lemon juice
1 teaspoon confectioners' sugar
1 lemon slice, for garnish

Place the gin, lemon juice, and confectioners' sugar in a cocktail shaker, fill it two-thirds of the way with ice, and shake until chilled.

Strain into a coupe, garnish with the lemon slice, and enjoy.

WHITE LADY

2 oz. gin
1 oz. Cointreau
½ oz. fresh lemon juice
Dash of egg white

Chill a cocktail glass in the freezer.

Place all of the ingredients in a cocktail shaker, fill it two-thirds of the way with ice, and shake until chilled.

Strain into the chilled cocktail glass and enjoy.

PINK GIN

1½ oz. gin
2 to 3 dashes of Angostura bitters
1 lemon peel
1 strip of lemon peel, for garnish

Fill a rocks glass with ice, add the gin and bitters, and stir until chilled.

Express the lemon peel over the cocktail so that the oil sits on top of the drink, garnish with the strip of lemon peel, and enjoy.

TROPICAL SLING PUNCH

2 oz. gin
½ oz. Cherry Heering
½ oz. Reàl Ginger Syrup
2 oz. fresh pineapple juice
½ oz. peach brandy
¾ oz. fresh lime juice
2 dashes of Angostura bitters
Club soda, to top
1 pineapple slice, for garnish
Fresh mint, for garnish
1 maraschino cherry, for garnish

Place all of the ingredients, except for the club soda and garnishes, in a cocktail shaker, fill it two-thirds of the way with ice, and shake until chilled.

Strain over crushed ice into a Hurricane glass and top with club soda.

Garnish with the slice of pineapple, fresh mint, and maraschino cherry and enjoy.

GREEN DRAGON

1½ oz. gin
½ oz. caraway liqueur
½ oz. green crème de menthe
1 oz. fresh lemon juice
4 dashes of orange bitters

Chill a cocktail glass in the freezer.

Place all of the ingredients in a cocktail shaker, fill it two-thirds of the way with ice, and shake until chilled.

Strain into the chilled cocktail glass and enjoy.

SUFFERING BASTARD

1 oz. London dry gin
1 oz. Cognac
⅔ oz. Lime Cordial (see recipe)
⅓ oz. fresh lime juice
3 dashes of Angostura bitters
3⅓ oz. ginger beer
1 pineapple wedge, for garnish
2 Luxardo maraschino cherries, for garnish
1 lime wedge, for garnish
Fresh mint, for garnish

Place all of the ingredients, except for the ginger beer and garnishes, in a cocktail shaker, fill it two-thirds of the way with ice, and shake until chilled.

Fill a Collins glass with crushed ice and strain the cocktail over it.

Top the cocktail with the ginger beer.

Garnish the cocktail with the pineapple wedge, cherries, lime wedge, and fresh mint and enjoy.

Lime Cordial: Rinse 18 limes with warm water and scrub them with your hands or a vegetable brush. Set them on a dish towel to dry. Peel the limes with a vegetable peeler, removing as little of the underlying white pith as possible. Place the peeled limes in the refrigerator to chill overnight. Place the peels in a nonreactive container and add 3 cups caster (superfine) sugar, making sure that it covers the peels entirely. Cover the container and let it rest overnight. The next day, cut the limes in half and juice them. Add the juice to the lime peel-and-sugar mixture and stir for several minutes, until the sugar has dissolved. Cover the container and refrigerate for at least 12 hours and up to 2 days. Strain the cordial through a fine sieve and chill in the refrigerator for 24 hours before using.

TOM COLLINS

One of history's most enduring cocktails, this archetypical highball was traditionally made using Old Tom gin, but when the citrus-forward flavor of London dry took a stranglehold on the market, the sweeter Old Tom was pushed to the brink of extinction. The Gin Renaissance, which occurred over the last few decades, brought Old Tom back, and it is highly recommended that you try the drink as it was originally intended to taste. After all, that recipe worked well enough to carry the Collins all the way from the early nineteenth century to the present.

Whichever gin you end up going with, make sure you adjust the amount of syrup in accordance with that particular gin's character. Also, don't be afraid to increase the amount of lemon juice if this recipe results in a drink that is just not quite as refreshing as it seems it should be. You also want the Tom Collins—and any fizz, really—to be as cold and undiluted as possible. To guarantee you check this box, fill the Collins glass with as much ice as you can, and consider chilling the glass in the freezer before straining the cocktail into it.

2 oz. Old Tom gin
1 oz. fresh lemon juice
½ oz. Rich Simple Syrup (see page 87)
2 oz. club soda
1 orange slice, for garnish
1 maraschino cherry, for garnish

Place the gin, lemon juice, and syrup in a cocktail shaker, fill it two-thirds of the way with ice, and shake until chilled.

Strain over ice into a Collins glass, top with the club soda, and gently stir to combine.

Garnish with the orange slice and maraschino cherry and enjoy.

GIN GREYHOUND

2 oz. gin

4 oz. grapefruit juice

1 sprig of fresh rosemary, for garnish

1 grapefruit twist, for garnish

Fill a highball glass with ice, add the gin, and top with the grapefruit juice.

Stir until chilled, garnish with the rosemary and grapefruit twist, and enjoy.

GIN FIZZ

1½ oz. gin

1 oz. fresh lemon juice

1 teaspoon confectioners' sugar

4 oz. club soda

Dash of grenadine

1 lemon slice, for garnish

Place the gin, lemon juice, and confectioners' sugar in a cocktail shaker, fill it two-thirds of the way with ice, and shake until chilled.

Strain the cocktail over ice into a highball glass and top with the club soda and grenadine.

Garnish with the lemon slice and enjoy.

MAIDEN'S PRAYER

1 oz. gin

1 oz. Lillet

1 oz. apple juice

Place all of the ingredients in a cocktail shaker, fill it two-thirds of the way with ice, and shake until chilled.

Strain over ice into a rocks glass and enjoy.

STRAWBERRY VINE

2 strawberries, hulled and sliced

2 oz. gin

½ oz. Simple Syrup **(see page 16)**

Juice of ½ lime

1 oz. club soda

1 sprig of fresh mint, for garnish

Place the strawberries in a highball glass, muddle, and fill the glass with ice.

Place the gin, syrup, and lime juice in a cocktail shaker, fill it two-thirds of the way with ice, and shake until chilled.

Strain into the glass, stir until combined, and top with the club soda.

Garnish with the fresh mint and enjoy.

HERBAL GIN & TONIC

HERBAL GIN & TONIC

2 oz. gin

Handful of fresh rosemary leaves

4 oz. tonic water

1 lime wheel, for garnish

1 lemon wheel, for garnish

1 sprig of fresh rosemary, for garnish

Place the gin and rosemary leaves in a cocktail shaker, fill it two-thirds of the way with ice, and shake until chilled.

Strain the cocktail over ice into a rocks glass and top with the tonic water.

Garnish with the lime wheel, lemon wheel, and fresh rosemary sprig and enjoy.

CLASSIC GIMLET

1½ oz. gin

½ oz. fresh lime juice

1 lime wedge, for garnish

Place the gin and lime juice in a cocktail shaker, fill it two-thirds of the way with ice, and shake until chilled.

Strain into a cocktail glass, garnish with the lime wedge, and enjoy.

SOUTH SIDE

2 oz. gin

Dash of limoncello

2 teaspoons caster (superfine) sugar

Juice of 1 lemon

4 fresh mint leaves, plus more for garnish

1 lemon slice, for garnish

Place the gin, limoncello, sugar, lemon juice, and fresh mint in a cocktail shaker, fill it two-thirds of the way with ice, and shake until chilled.

Strain the cocktail over ice into a mason jar, garnish with the lemon slice and additional fresh mint, and enjoy.

SUMMERTIME IS HERE

5 fresh mint leaves

1 oz. ginger ale

2 oz. lemonade

1 oz. gin

1 lemon wheel, for garnish

Tear the mint leaves in half and place them at the bottom of a highball glass.

Fill the glass with ice, add the ginger ale, lemonade, and gin, and stir until chilled.

Garnish with the lemon wheel and enjoy.

BLACKOUT

6 blackberries, plus more for garnish

4 fresh mint leaves

Dash of Simple Syrup (see page 16)

2 oz. gin

3 oz. lemonade

Dash of grenadine

Place the blackberries, fresh mint, and syrup in a cocktail shaker and muddle.

Add the gin, lemonade, grenadine, and ice and shake until chilled.

Strain the cocktail over ice into a highball glass, garnish with an additional blackberry, and enjoy.

GEORGIA ON MY MIND

4 oz. iced tea

2 oz. gin

2 oz. peach puree

1 teaspoon caster (superfine) sugar

2 to 3 peach wedges, for garnish

Place the iced tea, gin, peach puree, and sugar in a cocktail shaker, fill it two-thirds of the way with ice, and shake until chilled.

Strain the cocktail over ice into a Collins glass, garnish with the peach wedges, and enjoy.

STRAWBERRY & BASIL LEMONADE

1 strawberry, sliced

2 fresh basil leaves

2 oz. gin

Dash of strawberry vodka

3 oz. lemonade

Splash of club soda

1 strawberry, for garnish

Place the strawberry slices and basil leaves in a mason jar and muddle.

Add the gin, vodka, lemonade, and ice and stir until chilled.

Top with the club soda, garnish with the strawberry, and enjoy.

CRIMSON GARDEN

1½ oz. gin

½ oz. Rose Syrup (see recipe)

1 oz. fresh beet juice

½ oz. fresh lemon juice

1½ to 2 oz. Q Spectacular Tonic Water

1 thin slice of beet, for garnish

Edible rose petals, for garnish

Place all of the ingredients, except for the garnishes, in a cocktail shaker, fill it two-thirds of the way with ice, and shake until chilled.

Pour the contents of the shaker into a tumbler, garnish with the slice of beet and rose petals, and enjoy.

Rose Syrup: Place 1 cup rose water in a saucepan and bring to a boil. Add 1 cup sugar and stir until it has dissolved. Remove the pan from heat and let the syrup cool completely before using or storing in the refrigerator.

SALTY MUTT

Salt, for the rim
1 oz. gin
1 oz. grapefruit juice
1 oz. cranberry juice
1 grapefruit wedge, for garnish

Wet the rim of a rocks glass and rim it with salt.

Place the gin, grapefruit juice, and cranberry juice in a cocktail shaker, fill it two-thirds of the way with ice, and shake until chilled.

Fill the rimmed glass with ice and strain the cocktail over it.

Garnish with the grapefruit wedge and enjoy.

SINGAPORE EXPRESS

2 oz. gin
1 oz. cherry liqueur
1 oz. triple sec
3 oz. pineapple juice
1 maraschino cherry, for garnish
1 orange slice, for garnish

Place the gin, liqueur, triple sec, and pineapple juice in a cocktail shaker, fill it two-thirds of the way with ice, and shake until chilled.

Strain over ice into a Hurricane glass, garnish with the maraschino cherry and orange slice, and enjoy.

FRENCH NEGRONI

1½ oz. gin

1 oz. Suze

1 oz. sweet vermouth

1 orange wheel, for garnish

Fill a rocks glass with large ice cubes, add the gin, Suze, and vermouth, and stir until chilled.

Garnish with the orange wheel and enjoy.

ROSE WATER SOUR

2 oz. Hendrick's Gin

¾ oz. fresh lemon juice

¾ oz. Rose Water Mix (see recipe)

1 egg white

Drops of rose tincture, for garnish

Place all of the ingredients, except for the garnish, in a cocktail shaker and dry shake for 15 seconds.

Add ice and shake until chilled.

Strain into a coupe, garnish with a few drops of rose tincture, and enjoy.

Rose Water Mix: Combine 2 parts Red Wine Syrup (see recipe) with 1 part Combier Rose Liqueur and 1 part Orgeat (see page 103).

Red Wine Syrup: Combine equal parts caster (superfine) sugar and robust red wine and stir until the sugar has dissolved. Add cardamom tincture to taste and use or store in the refrigerator.

ROSE WATER SOUR

NEGRONI

A favorite of luminaries such as Ernest Hemingway, Orson Welles, and Anthony Bourdain and long treasured by bartenders everywhere, the Negroni currently carries as much clout as any classic cocktail. Thanks to its deep, appealing red coloring and the incomparable fusion of bitter, sweet, and woodsy flavors, you won't regret jumping on this bandwagon. As Kingsley Amis, the great English author and spirits aficionado (his *On Drink* is highly recommended, both for the humor and helpful tips), once said of the Negroni, "It has the power, rare with drinks and indeed with anything else, of cheering you up."

The canonical version of the drink is this drier rendition, which is better suited to the modern palate. But don't be afraid to experiment with the ratios, as the traditional preparation contained equal parts of the Campari, sweet vermouth, and gin. Just remain mindful that the herbal bite of the vermouth is there to build a bridge between the bittersweet Campari and the bold juniper kick of the gin. Don't hesitate to bounce back and forth between serving the cocktail up and on the rocks, as the changes in temperature will bring forth and mute different elements of the cocktail.

⅔ oz. Campari

⅔ oz. sweet vermouth

2 oz. gin

1 orange twist, for garnish

Fill a rocks glass with large ice cubes, add the Campari, sweet vermouth, and gin, and stir until chilled.

Garnish with the orange twist and enjoy.

VIOLET FIZZ

CLASSIC GIN & TONIC

2½ oz. gin
2½ oz. tonic water
Splash of fresh lime juice
1 lime wedge, for garnish

Fill a rocks glass with ice, add the gin and tonic water, and stir until chilled.

Top with the lime juice, garnish with the lime wedge, and enjoy.

VIOLET FIZZ

2 oz. gin
¾ oz. fresh lemon juice
½ oz. crème de violette
¼ oz. Orgeat (see page 103)
¼ oz. Rich Simple Syrup (see recipe)
½ oz. egg white
¼ oz. Passion Fruit Syrup (see recipe)
¼ oz. blue curaçao
1 oz. sparkling water, chilled

Place all of the ingredients, except for the sparkling water, in a cocktail shaker and dry shake for 10 seconds.

Add ice and shake until chilled.

Double strain over 2 ice cubes into a Collins glass, top with the sparkling water, and enjoy.

Rich Simple Syrup: Place 2 cups sugar and 1 cup water in a saucepan and bring it to a boil, stirring to dissolve the sugar. Remove the pan from heat and let the syrup cool completely before using or storing.

Passion Fruit Syrup: Place 1½ cups passion fruit puree and 1½ cups Demerara Syrup (see page 65) in a mason jar, seal it, and shake until combined. Use immediately or store in the refrigerator.

WAR OF THE ROSES

1 oz. gin

1 oz. triple sec

2 oz. club soda

Splash of grenadine

1 maraschino cherry, for garnish

Fill a rocks glass with ice, add the gin, triple sec, and club soda, and gently stir until chilled.

Top with the grenadine and let it filter through the cocktail.

Garnish with the maraschino cherry and enjoy.

GIN & JUICE

1 oz. gin

1 oz. cranberry juice

Splash of triple sec

Juice of ½ lime

1 lime wheel, for garnish

1 maraschino cherry, for garnish

Place the gin, cranberry juice, triple sec, and lime juice in a cocktail shaker, fill it two-thirds of the way with ice, and shake until chilled.

Strain over ice into a rocks glass, garnish with the lime wheel and maraschino cherry, and enjoy.

LONE STAR NEGRONI

1 strip of grapefruit peel

2 oz. Revolution Austin Reserve Gin, plus more to top

1 oz. Revolution Amico Amaro

1 oz. red vermouth

Rub the rim of a rocks glass with the grapefruit peel.

Place a large ice cube in the glass, add the gin, amaro, and vermouth, and stir until chilled.

Top with additional gin and enjoy.

CHERRY GIN SOUR

1 oz. gin

1 oz. cherry liqueur

1 oz. fresh lemon juice

Splash of Simple Syrup (see page 16)

1 maraschino cherry, for garnish

1 orange slice, for garnish

Place the gin, cherry liqueur, lemon juice, and syrup in a cocktail shaker, fill it two-thirds of the way with ice, and shake until chilled.

Strain over ice into a rocks glass, garnish with the maraschino cherry and orange slice, and enjoy.

THE BABY DILL

THE BABY DILL

2 cucumber slices, plus more for garnish

1 sprig of fresh dill

1¼ oz. New Western dry gin

¼ oz. Simple Syrup (see page 16)

¼ oz. fresh lemon juice

Chill a cocktail glass in the freezer.

Place the cucumber and dill in a cocktail shaker, add a bit of crushed ice, and muddle.

Add more ice and the remaining ingredients and shake until chilled.

Strain into the chilled cocktail glass, garnish with an additional cucumber slice, and enjoy.

TWISTED GIMLET

2 oz. gin

1 oz. triple sec

1 oz. fresh lime juice

2 drops of orange bitters

1 lime wheel, for garnish

Place the gin, triple sec, lime juice, and orange bitters in a cocktail shaker, fill it two-thirds of the way with ice, and shake until chilled.

Strain into a cocktail glass, garnish with the lime wheel, and enjoy.

PICASSO MARTINI

1 ice cube, made with dry vermouth

2 oz. gin

Chill a cocktail glass in the freezer.

Place the vermouth ice cube in the cocktail glass and add the gin.

Stir until chilled and enjoy.

GIN-GIN MULE

¾ oz. fresh lime juice

1 oz. Simple Syrup (see page 16)

1 sprig of fresh mint, plus more for garnish

1 oz. Homemade Ginger Beer (see recipe)

1¾ oz. London dry gin

1 lime wheel, for garnish

Crystallized ginger, for garnish

Place the lime juice, syrup, and fresh mint in a cocktail shaker and muddle.

Add the ginger beer, gin, and ice and shake vigorously until chilled.

Strain over ice into a Collins glass, garnish with additional fresh mint, the lime wheel, and crystallized ginger, and enjoy.

Homemade Ginger Beer: Place 1 gallon water in a large pot and bring to a boil. Add 1 cup of the boiling water to a food processor along with 1 lb. ginger. Blitz until the mixture is almost mulch-like. Place the ginger mixture in the boiling water, turn off the heat, and stir until well combined. Cover the pot and let the mixture steep for 1 hour. Strain the mixture through a fine-mesh sieve, pressing down on the ginger to extract as much liquid and flavor from it as possible. Stir in 4 oz. brown sugar and 2 oz. fresh lime juice and let the ginger beer cool before carbonating and storing in the refrigerator.

BRAMBLE

2 oz. gin
1 oz. fresh lemon juice
½ oz. Simple Syrup (see page 16)
½ oz. crème de mûre
1 raspberry or blackberry, for garnish

Place the gin, lemon juice, and syrup in a cocktail shaker, fill it two-thirds of the way with ice, and shake until chilled.

Fill a rocks glass with crushed ice and strain the cocktail over it.

Lace the crème de mûre on top of the cocktail, garnish with the blackberry or raspberry, and enjoy.

BREAKFAST MARTINI

1¾ oz. gin
1 bar spoon orange marmalade
½ oz. Cointreau
½ oz. fresh lemon juice
1 orange twist, for garnish

Place the gin and marmalade in a cocktail shaker and stir until well combined.

Add ice and the remaining ingredients, except for the garnish, and shake until chilled.

Strain into a cocktail glass, garnish with the orange twist, and enjoy.

SINGAPORE SLING

1½ oz. London dry gin
½ oz. Cherry Heering
¼ oz. Bénédictine
½ oz. fresh lemon juice
¼ oz. Demerara Syrup (see page 65)
Dash of Angostura bitters
Dash of orange bitters
Edible flower blossoms, for garnish

Place all of the ingredients, except for the garnish, in a cocktail shaker, fill it two-thirds of the way with ice, and shake until chilled.

Fill a Collins glass with crushed ice and strain the cocktail over it.

Garnish the cocktail with edible flowers and enjoy.

VERBENA

1¾ oz. Lemon Verbena–Infused Gin (see recipe)
1 teaspoon Lavender Syrup (see recipe)
2 teaspoons Velvet Falernum
1 oz. apple juice

Fill a rocks glass with ice, add all of the ingredients, stir until chilled, and enjoy.

Lemon Verbena–Infused Gin: Combine 1 liter gin and ¼ cup fresh lemon verbena leaves in a large mason jar, let the mixture steep for 24 hours to 4 days, and strain before using.

Lavender Syrup: Prepare Simple Syrup (see page 16) in a medium saucepan. While the syrup is boiling, add 2 tablespoons dried lavender leaves, remove the pan from heat, and let the syrup cool completely. Strain before using or storing.

SINGAPORE SLING

ASYLUM HARBOR

ASYLUM HARBOR

1¼ oz. Damrak Gin
½ oz. Bénédictine
¼ oz. almond liqueur
1 bar spoon St. Elizabeth Allspice Dram
½ oz. Ginger Syrup (see recipe)
½ oz. passion fruit puree
½ oz. fresh lime juice
¾ oz. grapefruit juice
Peychaud's bitters, for garnish
Freshly grated nutmeg, for garnish
Fresh mint, for garnish
1 grapefruit twist, for garnish

Place all of the ingredients, except for the garnishes, in a cocktail shaker, fill it two-thirds of the way with ice, and shake until chilled.

Strain over ice into a Collins glass, garnish with the bitters, nutmeg, fresh mint, and grapefruit twist, and enjoy.

Ginger Syrup: Place 1 cup water and 1 cup sugar in a saucepan and bring the mixture to a boil, stirring to dissolve the sugar. Add a peeled 1-inch piece of fresh ginger, remove the pan from heat, and let the syrup cool completely. Strain before using or storing.

VESPER MARTINI

3 oz. gin
1 oz. vodka
½ oz. Lillet Blanc
1 strip of lemon peel, for garnish

Place the gin, vodka, and Lillet in a cocktail shaker, fill it two-thirds of the way with ice, and shake until chilled.

Strain into a cocktail glass, garnish with the strip of lemon peel, and enjoy.

CHASING WATERFALLS

1 oz. gin
1 oz. Champagne
2 oz. Sprite
Juice of ½ lemon
1 lemon wheel, for garnish

Place the gin, Champagne, Sprite, and lemon juice in a highball glass, add ice, and gently stir to combine.

Garnish with the lemon wheel and enjoy.

WAKEUP MARTINI

2 oz. gin
1 oz. triple sec
Splash of fresh lemon juice
Splash of maple syrup
1 lemon twist, for garnish

Place the gin, triple sec, lemon juice, and maple syrup in a cocktail shaker, fill it two-thirds of the way with ice, and shake until chilled.

Strain into a cocktail glass, garnish with the lemon twist, and enjoy.

THE FORUM

1½ oz. gin
2 teaspoons Noilly Prat Dry Vermouth
4 to 5 drops of Grand Marnier

Chill a cocktail glass in the freezer.

Place all of the ingredients in a mixing glass, fill it two-thirds of the way with ice, and stir until chilled.

Strain into the chilled cocktail glass and enjoy.

PURPLE SKY

1½ oz. gin

½ oz. fresh lemon juice

2 dashes of crème de violette

½ oz. Luxardo maraschino liqueur

Chill a cocktail glass in the freezer.

Place all of the ingredients in a cocktail shaker, fill it two-thirds of the way with ice, and shake until chilled.

Strain into the chilled cocktail glass and enjoy.

THE SOIREE

2 oz. Audemus Pink Pepper Gin

1 oz. Giffard Crème de Pamplemousse Rose

Juice of ½ lemon

2 to 4 pink peppercorns, for garnish

1 lemon twist, for garnish

Chill a coupe in the freezer.

Place the gin, liqueur, and lemon juice in a mixing glass, fill it two-thirds of the way with ice, and stir until chilled.

Strain into the chilled coupe, garnish with the peppercorns and lemon twist, and enjoy.

FRENCH 75

1 sugar cube
Juice of 1 lemon wedge
1 oz. gin
2 oz. Champagne
1 lemon twist, for garnish
1 Luxardo maraschino cherry, skewered, for garnish

Place the sugar cube in a Champagne flute, add the lemon juice and gin, and top with the Champagne.

Stir to combine, garnish with the lemon twist and maraschino cherry, and enjoy.

LEA D'ASCO

½ oz. Beefeater London Dry Gin
1 oz. Lillet
½ oz. whiskey
½ oz. absinthe
1 strip of orange peel, for garnish

Chill a cocktail glass in the freezer.

Place the gin, Lillet, whiskey, and absinthe in a mixing glass, fill it two-thirds of the way with ice, and stir until chilled.

Strain into the chilled cocktail glass, garnish with the strip of orange peel, and enjoy.

ROSEBUD

¼ oz. Hendrick's Gin

¼ oz. sweet vermouth

½ oz. Combier Crème de Rose

½ oz. Simple Syrup (see page 16)

½ oz. fresh lemon juice

2 dashes of cranberry bitters

Tonic water, to top

Place the gin, vermouth, liqueur, syrup, lemon juice, and bitters in a cocktail shaker, fill it two-thirds of the way with ice, and shake until chilled.

Strain over ice into a highball glass, top with tonic water, and enjoy.

SNOW BOWL

1 oz. gin

1 oz. white chocolate liqueur

Splash of white crème de menthe

Freshly grated nutmeg, for garnish

Place the gin, liqueur, and crème de menthe in a cocktail shaker, fill it two-thirds of the way with ice, and shake until chilled.

Strain over ice into a rocks glass, garnish with a dusting of nutmeg, and enjoy.

SLEEPING LOTUS

3 fresh mint leaves, plus more for garnish

2 oz. gin

1 oz. Orgeat (see recipe)

¾ oz. fresh lemon juice

2 dashes of orange bitters

1 edible flower blossom, for garnish

Place the fresh mint in a cocktail shaker and muddle.

Add ice and the remaining ingredients, except for the garnish, and shake until chilled.

Fill a Collins glass with crushed ice and double strain the cocktail over it.

Garnish with additional fresh mint and the edible flower blossom and enjoy.

Orgeat: Preheat the oven to 400°F. Place 2 cups almonds on a baking sheet, place them in the oven, and toast until they are fragrant, about 5 minutes. Remove the almonds from the oven and let them cool completely. Place the almonds in a food processor and pulse until they are a coarse meal. Set the almonds aside. Place 1 cup Demerara Syrup (see page 65) in a saucepan and warm it over medium heat. Add the almond meal, remove the pan from heat, and let the mixture steep for 6 hours. Strain the mixture through cheesecloth and discard the solids. Stir in 1 teaspoon orange blossom water and 2 oz. vodka and use immediately or store in the refrigerator.

THE CHURCH

THE CHURCH

1 oz. Aperol

1 oz. London dry gin

1 oz. fresh lemon juice

½ oz. Demerara Syrup (see page 65)

½ oz. Cocchi Americano

1 long strip of orange peel, for garnish

Place all of the ingredients, except for the garnish, in a cocktail shaker, fill it two-thirds of the way with ice, and shake until chilled.

Double strain the cocktail over a large ice cube into a double rocks glass, garnish with the strip of orange peel, and enjoy.

LE PULPEUX

1½ oz. Beefeater London Dry Gin

½ oz. thyme liqueur

½ oz. grapefruit juice

½ oz. fresh lime juice

Ginger beer, to top

Place the gin, liqueur, grapefruit juice, and lime juice in a cocktail shaker, fill it two-thirds of the way with ice, and shake until chilled.

Strain over ice into a highball glass, top with ginger beer, and enjoy.

BIJOU COCKTAIL

1½ oz. London dry gin
¾ oz. sweet vermouth
¾ oz. Green Chartreuse
Dash of orange bitters
1 strip of lemon peel, for garnish

Chill a coupe in the freezer.

Place the gin, vermouth, Chartreuse, and bitters in a mixing glass, fill it two-thirds of the way with ice, and stir until chilled.

Strain into the chilled coupe, garnish with the strip of lemon peel, and enjoy.

FRENCH 75 SQUARED

2 oz. gin
1 oz. fresh lemon juice
1 teaspoon caster (superfine) sugar
1 oz. St-Germain
Champagne, to top
2 Luxardo maraschino cherries, for garnish

Chill a coupe in the freezer.

Place the gin, lemon juice, sugar, and St-Germain in a cocktail shaker, fill it two-thirds of the way with ice, and shake until chilled.

Strain into the chilled coupe and top with Champagne.

Skewer the cherries on a toothpick, garnish the cocktail with them, and enjoy.

VICE VERSA

¾ oz. grapefruit juice

½ oz. Luxardo Bitter

½ oz. Giffard Crème de Pamplemousse Rose

1 oz. New York Distilling Co. Dorothy Parker Gin

Rosé Cava, to top

Place the grapefruit juice, bitters, liqueur, and gin in a cocktail shaker, fill it two-thirds of the way with ice, and shake until chilled.

Strain into a large coupe, top with rosé Cava, and enjoy.

OBITUARY

2 oz. gin

1 oz. dry vermouth

1 bar spoon absinthe

1 lemon twist, for garnish

Chill a cocktail glass in the freezer.

Place the gin, vermouth, and absinthe in a mixing glass, fill it two-thirds of the way with ice, and stir until chilled.

Strain into the chilled cocktail glass, garnish with the lemon twist, and enjoy.

HANKY PANKY

1½ oz. gin

1 oz. sweet vermouth

2 dashes of Fernet-Branca

1 orange twist, for garnish

Place the gin, vermouth, and Fernet-Branca in a mixing glass, fill it two-thirds of the way with ice, and stir until chilled.

Strain into a coupe, garnish with the orange twist, and enjoy.

THE MISSIONARY

1½ oz. gin

1 oz. Mixed Berry Shrub (see recipe)

¾ oz. grapefruit juice

2 cucumbers, chopped

1 grapefruit peel strip, for garnish

Place the gin, Mixed Berry Shrub, grapefruit juice, and cucumbers in a cocktail shaker, fill it two-thirds of the way with ice, and shake until chilled.

Strain over ice into a rocks glass, garnish with the grapefruit peel strip, and enjoy.

Mixed Berry Shrub: Place ½ cup apple cider vinegar, ½ cup sugar, and ¼ cup frozen mixed berries in a saucepan and bring to a boil, mashing the berries with a wooden spoon and stirring to dissolve the sugar. Cook for 5 minutes, remove the pan from heat, and let the shrub cool completely. Strain before using or storing.

HANKY PANKY

JOY DIVISION

2 oz. Beefeater London Dry Gin
1 oz. Dolin Blanc Vermouth
½ oz. triple sec or Cointreau
3 dashes of absinthe
1 lemon twist, for garnish

Place the gin, vermouth, triple sec, and absinthe in a mixing glass, fill it two-thirds of the way with ice, and stir until chilled.

Strain into a coupe, garnish with the lemon twist, and enjoy.

GARDEN PARTY

¾ oz. fresh lemon juice
½ oz. Simple Syrup (see page 16)
2 strips of red bell pepper
2 oz. gin
¾ oz. Aperol
Pinch of black pepper, for garnish

Place the lemon juice, syrup, and bell pepper in a cocktail shaker and muddle.

Add the gin, Aperol, and ice and shake until chilled.

Strain into a coupe, garnish with the black pepper, and enjoy.

CORPSE REVIVER NO. 2

¾ oz. London dry gin

¾ oz. fresh lemon juice

¾ oz. Cointreau

¾ oz. Cocchi Americano

1 teaspoon absinthe

1 lemon twist, for garnish

Place the gin, lemon juice, Cointreau, Cocchi Americano, and absinthe in a cocktail shaker, fill it two-thirds of the way with ice, and shake until chilled.

Strain into a coupe, garnish with the lemon twist, and enjoy.

WOOLYNESIA

1½ oz. Old Tom gin

¾ oz. Ancho Reyes Verde Chile Poblano Liqueur

1 oz. fresh lime juice

½ oz. Aperol

½ oz. passion fruit juice

1 teaspoon grated ginger

1 teaspoon cinnamon

1 teaspoon Giffard Crème de Pêche de Vigne

1 sprig of fresh mint, for garnish

Place the gin, liqueur, lime juice, Aperol, passion fruit juice, ginger, cinnamon, and Crème de Pêche de Vigne in a cocktail shaker and dry shake for 10 to 15 seconds.

Add ice and shake until chilled.

Strain over pebble ice into a tiki mug, garnish with the fresh mint, and enjoy.

DIRTY MARTINI

THE BRONX COCKTAIL

1½ oz. London dry gin
½ oz. sweet vermouth
½ oz. extra-dry vermouth
1 oz. fresh orange juice
Dash of Regans' Orange Bitters No. 6 (optional)
1 strip of orange peel, for garnish

Chill a cocktail glass in the freezer.

Place the gin, sweet vermouth, extra-dry vermouth, orange juice, and bitters (if using) in a cocktail shaker, fill it two-thirds of the way with ice, and shake until chilled.

Strain into the chilled cocktail glass, garnish with the strip of orange peel, and enjoy.

DIRTY MARTINI

4 oz. gin
1 oz. dry vermouth
Splash of olive brine
3 pimento-stuffed olives, for garnish

Chill a cocktail glass in the freezer.

Place the gin, vermouth, and olive brine in a mixing glass, fill it two-thirds of the way with ice, and stir until chilled.

Strain into the chilled cocktail glass, skewer the olives on a toothpick, garnish the cocktail with them, and enjoy.

GIN BASIL SMASH

½ oz. Liber & Co. Classic Gum Syrup

9 fresh basil leaves, plus more for garnish

2 oz. gin

¾ oz. fresh lemon juice

Place the syrup and basil leaves in a cocktail shaker and muddle.

Add the gin, lemon juice, and ice and shake until chilled.

Double strain over ice into a rocks glass, garnish with additional basil, and enjoy.

GIN 'N' ROSES

1 oz. Martin Miller's Gin

1 oz. Cocchi Rosa Americano

½ oz. fresh lemon juice

½ oz. Giffard Black Rose Liqueur

¼ oz. Honey Syrup (see page 64)

Dried rosebuds, for garnish

Place the gin, Cocchi Rosa Americano, lemon juice, liqueur, and syrup in a cocktail shaker, fill it two-thirds of the way with ice, and shake until chilled.

Strain over ice into a rocks glass, garnish with the dried rosebuds, and enjoy.

GIN GRIN

½ lemon
1½ oz. gin
½ oz. Aperol
¾ oz. Simple Syrup (see page 16)
2 dashes of Angostura bitters
5 to 6 fresh mint leaves, plus more for garnish

Place the lemon in a cocktail shaker and muddle.

Add ice and all of the remaining ingredients and shake vigorously for 5 minutes.

Strain over ice into a rocks glass and top with cracked ice.

Garnish with additional mint and enjoy.

PRELUDE TO A KISS

1½ oz. Empress 1908 Gin
¾ oz. fresh lime juice
½ oz. Dolin Blanc Vermouth
¼ oz. Chambord
½ oz. crème de violette
½ oz. Lavender Syrup (see page 94)
½ oz. egg white

Place all of the ingredients in a cocktail shaker and dry shake for 10 seconds.

Add ice to the shaker and shake until chilled.

Double strain the cocktail into a coupe and enjoy.

WHITE NEGRONI

1 oz. Domaine de Canton ginger liqueur

1 oz. Grand Marnier

1½ oz. gin

1 lemon twist, for garnish

Place all of the ingredients, except for the garnish, in a mixing glass, fill it two-thirds of the way with ice, and stir until chilled.

Strain over an ice sphere into a rocks glass, garnish with the lemon twist, and enjoy.

OLIVETO

2 oz. London dry gin

⅘ oz. fresh lemon juice

⅖ oz. Rich Simple Syrup (see page 87)

⅖ oz. Licor 43

½ oz. extra-virgin olive oil

1 egg white

Place all of the ingredients in a cocktail shaker, add 3 ice cubes, and shake until the ice has almost completely dissolved.

Strain the cocktail into a stemless wineglass and enjoy.

WHITE NEGRONI

THE FLEUR DU MAL

1 oz. gin
1 oz. Lillet
1 oz. St-Germain
½ oz. fresh lemon juice
½ oz. grapefruit juice
¼ oz. grenadine
¼ oz. tonic water
Orange blossom water, to spritz
Dried rosebuds, for garnish

Place the gin, Lillet, St-Germain, lemon juice, grapefruit juice, grenadine, and tonic water in a cocktail shaker, fill it two-thirds of the way with ice, and shake until chilled.

Double strain into a coupe and spritz the cocktail with orange blossom water.

Garnish with the dried rosebuds and enjoy.

CORPSE IMBIBER

Absinthe, to mist
1½ oz. London dry gin
¾ oz. Cocchi Rosa Americano
¾ oz. fresh grapefruit juice
¼ oz. fresh lemon juice
¾ oz. Tempus Fugit Spirits Gran Classico Bitter
1 strip of grapefruit peel, for garnish

Mist a coupe with absinthe.

Place the gin, Cocchi Rosa, grapefruit juice, lemon juice, and Gran Classico in a cocktail shaker, fill it two-thirds of the way with ice, and shake until chilled.

Strain into the coupe, garnish with the strip of grapefruit peel, and enjoy.

THYME TRAVELER

1 cucumber ribbon

1½ oz. Bombay Dry Gin

½ oz. St-Germain

¾ oz. freshly pressed cucumber juice

½ oz. Thyme Syrup (see recipe)

½ oz. fresh lemon juice

Dash of Bittermens Hellfire Habanero Shrub

1 sprig of fresh thyme, for garnish

Place all of the ingredients, except for the thyme, in a cocktail shaker, fill it two-thirds of the way with ice, and shake until chilled.

Strain over ice into a Collins glass, garnish with the fresh thyme, and enjoy.

Thyme Syrup: Place 1 cup water, 1 cup sugar, and 1 small bundle of fresh thyme in a saucepan and bring to a boil, stirring to dissolve the sugar. Remove the pan from heat and let the mixture steep for 1 hour. Strain and let the syrup cool completely before using or storing.

THE CLOVER CLUB

1½ oz. London dry gin
½ oz. dry vermouth
½ oz. fresh lemon juice
½ oz. Raspberry Syrup (see page 22)
½ oz. egg white
3 raspberries, for garnish

Place the gin, vermouth, lemon juice, syrup, and egg white in a cocktail shaker and dry shake for 10 to 15 seconds.

Add ice and shake until chilled.

Strain into a coupe, skewer the raspberries on a toothpick, garnish the cocktail with them, and enjoy.

PERFECT MARTINI

2½ oz. gin
½ oz. dry vermouth
½ oz. sweet vermouth
1 lemon twist, for garnish

Chill a cocktail glass in the freezer.

Place the gin, dry vermouth, and sweet vermouth in a mixing glass, fill it two-thirds of the way with ice, and stir until chilled.

Strain into the chilled cocktail glass, garnish with the lemon twist, and enjoy.

THE CLOVER CLUB

RAMOS GIN FIZZ

2 oz. gin

1 oz. half-and-half

¾ oz. Simple Syrup (see page 16)

½ oz. fresh lemon juice

½ oz. fresh lime juice

2 dashes of orange blossom water

1 egg white

Club soda, to top

1 orange twist, for garnish

Chill a Collins glass in the freezer.

Place all of the ingredients, except for the club soda and garnish, in a cocktail shaker and dry shake for 15 seconds.

Fill the shaker one-quarter of the way with ice and shake for 3 minutes.

Pour the cocktail into the chilled glass, top with club soda, garnish with the orange twist, and enjoy.

BEE'S KNEES

2 oz. London dry gin
¾ oz. fresh lemon juice
¾ oz. Honey Syrup (see page 64)
1 lemon twist, for garnish

Chill a coupe in the freezer.

Place the gin, lemon juice, and syrup in a cocktail shaker, fill it two-thirds of the way with ice, and shake until chilled.

Strain into the chilled coupe, garnish with the lemon twist, and enjoy.

COOL LAGOON

6 fresh Thai basil leaves, plus more for garnish
Handful of fresh Italian basil leaves
1 oz. Pickled Jalapeño Syrup (see recipe)
1½ oz. London dry gin
1 oz. Italicus Rosolio di Bergamotto
⅓ oz. Pavan liqueur
Dash of The Bitter Truth Cucumber Bitters
Frozen green grapes, for garnish

Place the basil leaves in a cocktail shaker and muddle.

Add the syrup, gin, liqueurs, bitters, and ice and shake until chilled.

Strain over ice into a rocks glass, garnish with the frozen grapes and additional basil, and enjoy.

Pickled Jalapeño Syrup: Prepare Simple Syrup (see page 16) in a medium saucepan. When the syrup comes to a boil, add 5 slices of pickled jalapeño pepper and a dash of the pickled jalapeño brine, remove the pan from heat, and let it cool completely. Strain before using or storing.

HUSK FIZZ

¾ oz. Coriander Syrup (see recipe)
1½ oz. London dry gin
½ oz. fresh lime juice
¾ oz. coconut milk
½ makrut lime leaf, torn, plus more for garnish
Club soda, chilled, to top
Orange blossom water, to spritz

Chill a Collins glass in the freezer.

Place the syrup, gin, lime juice, coconut milk, and lime leaf in a cocktail shaker, fill it two-thirds of the way with ice, and shake until chilled.

Strain into the chilled Collins glass and top with club soda.

Spritz with orange blossom water, garnish with an additional lime leaf, and enjoy.

Coriander Syrup: Prepare Simple Syrup (see page 16) in a medium saucepan. While the syrup is boiling, add ½ cup coriander seeds, remove the pan from heat, and let it cool completely. Strain before using or storing.

TEQUILA & MEZCAL

When using tequila in a cocktail, there's really only one rule that you need to adhere to: do not use any expression that is less than 100 percent blue agave—the impure iterations are also known as mixtos. Since they are cheaper to produce, there are many more mixto brands on the market than there are pure agave brands. Legally, these mixto tequilas must be made with at least 51 percent pure blue agave sugar. The other portion of the sugars can be from non-agave sources, like sugarcane, which will affect the taste of the spirit in a negative fashion.

Mezcal is a little different—since it is far more of a craft spirit than tequila, meaning that you can expect a wide range of flavors among the various producers and expressions. That's not to say you shouldn't feel free to try mixing any mezcal you enjoy, but Del Maguey's Vida offering is a good default option, since it was designed in response to bartenders asking the company to make something that was more amenable to crafting cocktails.

EARLY NIGHT

1 oz. tequila

1 oz. Luxardo maraschino liqueur

Juice of ½ lime

2 oz. orange juice

1 maraschino cherry, for garnish

Fill a highball glass with ice, add the tequila, Luxardo, and juices, and stir until chilled.

Garnish with the maraschino cherry and enjoy.

KINDA KNEW ANNA

1 oz. tequila

1 oz. crème de mûre

1 oz. fresh lime juice

2 oz. ginger beer

1 fresh sage leaf, for garnish

Place the tequila, liqueur, and lime juice in a cocktail shaker, fill it two-thirds of the way with ice, and shake until chilled.

Strain over ice into a double rocks glass, top with the ginger beer, and garnish with the sage leaf.

THE TEQUILA DAISY

2 oz. tequila
1 oz. fresh lemon juice
½ oz. grenadine
½ oz. Simple Syrup (see page 16)
Splash of seltzer water

Place the tequila, lemon juice, grenadine, and syrup in a cocktail shaker, fill it two-thirds of the way with ice, and shake until chilled.

Strain into a coupe, top with the seltzer, and enjoy.

FROZEN PINEAPPLE MARGARITA

Salt, for the rim
2 oz. tequila
1 oz. mezcal
3 oz. pineapple juice
1 cup crushed ice
¼ cup chopped pineapple
1½ oz. orange liqueur
2 oz. fresh lime juice
1 lime wedge, for garnish

Wet the rim of a large coupe and rim it with salt.

Place the tequila, mezcal, pineapple juice, crushed ice, pineapple, liqueur, and lime juice in a blender and pulse until smooth.

Pour into the rimmed coupe, garnish with the lime wedge, and enjoy.

MARGARITA

Sometimes three is not a crowd, but the magic number. The base of the Margarita—tequila, orange liqueur, and lime juice—is one such example. The Margarita is a riff on the Daisy, a cocktail that was popular during the 1930s and '40s. The connection becomes clear when one realizes that margarita is the Spanish word for "daisy." While much debate rages over who came up with the cocktail, its pleasant taste and unquestioned status as the signal that it's time to let the good times roll has made it the most popular cocktail in America.

As with many classic cocktails, the foundational simplicity obscures how much room there is for experimentation. One of the most popular tweaks, so beloved its devotees believe it to be the only acceptable version, is the Tommy's Margarita, which consists of 2 oz. silver tequila, 1 oz. fresh lime juice, and ½ oz. agave nectar. Whether you follow that example and simplify, swap one of the ingredients suggested below for something else, or try to incorporate a favored ingredient, the most important thing when mixing up a Margarita is to make it wholly yours.

Salt, for the rim
2 oz. silver tequila
½ oz. Cointreau
1 oz. fresh lime juice
½ oz. Simple Syrup (see page 16)
3 dashes of 10 Percent Saline Solution (see page 64)
1 lime wedge, for garnish

Wet the rim of a rocks glass and rim it with salt.

Place all of the remaining ingredients, except for the garnish, in a cocktail shaker, fill it two-thirds of the way with ice, and shake until chilled.

Pour the cocktail into the rimmed glass, add more ice if desired, garnish with the lime wedge, and enjoy.

BLANCO
Tequila
CÓDIGO
1530
BLANCO

TEX-MEX MULE

2½ oz. reposado tequila

2 oz. fresh lime juice

½ oz. Domaine de Canton ginger liqueur

½ oz. orange liqueur

5 oz. ginger beer

1 lime wedge, for garnish

Place the tequila, lime juice, liqueurs, and ginger beer in a cocktail shaker, fill it two-thirds of the way with ice, and shake until chilled.

Strain over ice into a copper mug, garnish with the lime wedge, and enjoy.

THINK PINK

Pink Himalayan or Hawaiian sea salt, for the rim

2 oz. tequila

1 oz. fresh lime juice

1 oz. fresh ruby red grapefruit juice

¾ oz. Simple Syrup (see page 16)

1 oz. orange liqueur

3 oz. sparkling rosé

1 lime wedge, for garnish

Wet the rim of a rocks glass and rim it with salt.

Place the tequila, juices, syrup, and liqueur in a cocktail shaker, fill it two-thirds of the way with ice, and shake until chilled.

Strain into the rocks glass and top with the rosé.

Garnish with the lime wedge and enjoy.

VAMPIRO

Tajín, for the rim

2 oz. mezcal

2 oz. Vampiro Mix (see recipe)

½ oz. fresh lime juice

2 oz. fresh grapefruit juice

¾ oz. Simple Syrup (see page 16)

Pinch of kosher salt

2 oz. seltzer water

1 dehydrated blood orange wheel, for garnish

Wet the rim of a Collins glass and rim half of it with Tajín.

Place the mezcal, Vampiro Mix, juices, and syrup in a cocktail shaker, add 1 ice cube, and whip shake until chilled.

Pour the cocktail into the rimmed glass, add the salt and seltzer, garnish with the dehydrated blood orange wheel, and enjoy.

Vampiro Mix: Place 1¼ cups Clamato, 2 tablespoons apple cider vinegar, 6 tablespoons fresh lime juice, ¼ cup agave nectar, 1 tablespoon sriracha, 2 teaspoons blood orange juice, 2 teaspoons smoked paprika, and 1 teaspoon ground black pepper in a blender, add salt to taste, and pulse until combined. Use as desired.

ÚLTIMA PALABRA

¾ oz. mezcal

¾ oz. Green Chartreuse

¾ oz. Luxardo maraschino liqueur

¾ oz. fresh lime juice

Place the mezcal, liqueurs, and lime juice in a cocktail shaker, fill it two-thirds of the way with ice, and shake until chilled.

Double strain into a coupe and enjoy.

EAST LA

Tajín, for the rim

4 to 5 cucumber slices, plus more for garnish

1 oz. fresh key lime juice

2 oz. tequila

¾ oz. Simple Syrup (see page 16)

8 fresh mint leaves

3 dashes of 10 Percent Saline Solution (see page 64)

Wet the rim of a double rocks glass and rim half of it with Tajín. Add ice to the glass.

Place the cucumber and key lime juice in a cocktail shaker and muddle.

Add the tequila and syrup, give the mint leaves a smack, and drop them into the shaker. Fill it two-thirds of the way with ice, add the saline solution, and shake until chilled.

Double strain into the rimmed glass, garnish with an additional slice of cucumber, and enjoy.

MEZCAL & MANGO FLOAT

1 cup mango puree

1 cup ginger beer

2 oz. mezcal

3 to 4 scoops of vanilla ice cream

Place the puree, ginger beer, and mezcal in a large mason jar and stir to combine.

Place the ice cream in a separate mason jar and pour the mango soda over the top. Enjoy immediately.

RAMON BRAVO

Salt, for the rim

1½ oz. Chorizo-Washed Mezcal (see recipe)

½ oz. Ancho Reyes liqueur

1 oz. Charred Pineapple Puree (see recipe)

1 oz. fresh lime juice

¾ oz. Ginger & Serrano Syrup (see recipe)

4 sprigs of fresh cilantro

Wet the rim of a highball glass and rim it with salt.

Place all of the remaining ingredients in a cocktail shaker, fill it two-thirds of the way with ice, and shake until chilled.

Strain into the rimmed glass and enjoy.

Chorizo-Washed Mezcal: Remove the casing from ½ lb. Mexican chorizo, place the chorizo in a dry skillet, and cook over low heat to render the fat. When the chorizo is cooked through, remove it from the pan and use it in another preparation. Place the rendered fat in a large mason jar. For every 2 oz. of fat, add a 750 ml bottle of mezcal. Let the mixture sit at room temperature for 12 hours. Chill the mixture in the freezer for 6 to 8 hours. Strain the mezcal through a fine-mesh sieve or cheesecloth and use as desired.

Charred Pineapple Puree: Prepare a gas or charcoal grill for medium heat (about 400°F). Peel a pineapple, core it, and slice it into rings. Place the pineapple on the grill and cook until it is charred on both sides, about 6 minutes, turning it as necessary. Place the pineapple in a blender and pulse, adding water 1 tablespoon at a time until the texture of the puree is similar to applesauce. Use as desired.

Ginger & Serrano Syrup: Place 1 cup sugar, ½ cup water, and 3 stemmed and seeded serrano chile peppers in a saucepan. Chop 2 large pieces of fresh ginger, add them to the pan, and bring to a boil, stirring to dissolve the sugar. Remove the pan from heat and let the syrup cool completely. Strain before using or storing.

125
YEARS
AGUA
MINERAL
Topo Chico
CIA TOPO CHICO
MINERAL WATER
CARBONATED
12 FL OZ

RANCH WATER

RANCH WATER

Salt, for the rim, plus more to taste

2 oz. silver tequila

½ oz. fresh lime juice

4 oz. Topo Chico

1 lime wedge, for garnish

Wet the rim of a highball glass and rim it with salt. Add ice to the glass along with the tequila and lime juice.

Top with the Top Chico, add a pinch of salt, and gently stir.

Garnish with the lime wedge and enjoy.

BATANGA

2 pinches of kosher salt, plus more for the rim

½ oz. fresh lime juice

2 oz. silver tequila

3½ oz. Mexican Coca-Cola

1 lime wedge, for garnish

Wet the rim of a highball glass and rim it with salt.

Place the lime juice and salt in the glass and stir until the salt has dissolved.

Add the tequila and ice, top with the cola, and gently stir to combine.

Garnish with the lime wedge and enjoy.

PLAYA ROSITA

¾ oz. reposado tequila

¾ oz. mezcal

½ oz. Pineapple-Infused Campari (see recipe)

½ oz. sweet vermouth

½ oz. dry vermouth

Dash of Bittermens 'Elemakule Tiki Bitters

1 orange twist, for garnish

Combine all of the ingredients, except for the garnish, in a mixing glass, fill it two-thirds of the way with ice, and stir until chilled.

Strain into a cocktail glass, garnish with the orange twist, and enjoy.

Pineapple-Infused Campari: Place ¾ lb. finely diced pineapple and 1½ cups Campari in a large container and let the mixture steep for 24 to 48 hours. Strain and use as desired.

THE HIGH ROLLER

Flaky sea salt, for the rim

2 oz. premium silver tequila

1 oz. Grand Marnier

1 oz. fresh lime juice

1 split of Champagne

1 lime twist, for garnish

Wet the rim of a rocks glass and rim it with salt.

Place the tequila, Grand Marnier, and lime juice in a cocktail shaker, fill it two-thirds of the way with ice, and shake until chilled.

Strain over ice into the rocks glass and carefully flip the split of Champagne into the glass.

Garnish with the lime twist and enjoy.

OAXACA OLD FASHIONED

1½ oz. tequila

½ oz. mezcal

2 dashes of Angostura bitters

1 bar spoon agave nectar

1 strip of orange peel, torched, for garnish

Place all of the ingredients, except for the garnish, in a mixing glass, fill it two-thirds of the way with ice, and stir until chilled.

Strain into a rocks glass, garnish with the torched orange peel, and enjoy.

OAXACARAJILLO

1½ oz. Licor 43

1 oz. mezcal

1 bar spoon agave nectar

1 oz. freshly brewed espresso, cooled slightly

Add the Licor 43, mezcal, and agave nectar to a double rocks glass.

Add 1 large ice cube. Slowly pour the espresso over the back of a bar spoon, positioned as close to the cube as possible, so that it floats atop the cocktail. Enjoy immediately.

COOPER'S CAFÉ

1 oz. freshly brewed espresso

2 oz. mezcal

½ oz. Cinnamon Syrup (see page 262)

1 strip of orange peel, for garnish

Place the espresso, mezcal, and syrup in a cocktail shaker, fill it two-thirds of the way with ice, and shake until chilled.

Strain into a Nick & Nora glass, garnish with the strip of orange peel, and enjoy.

CARAJILLO

1 oz. Licor 43

1 oz. reposado tequila

1½ oz. freshly brewed espresso

Place the Licor 43, tequila, and espresso in a cocktail shaker, fill it two-thirds of the way with ice, and shake until chilled.

Strain over a large ice cube into a rocks glass and enjoy.

CANOE CLUB

1½ oz. mezcal

½ oz. crème de mûre

¾ oz. Ginger & Serrano Syrup (see page 135)

½ oz. fresh lime juice

3 dashes of Peychaud's bitters

Place all of the ingredients in a cocktail shaker and stir to combine. Fill the shaker two-thirds of the way with ice and shake until chilled.

Strain over ice into a rocks glass and enjoy.

THE BLACKER THE BERRY, THE SWEETER THE JUICE

5 blackberries

1½ oz. mezcal

¾ oz. St-Germain

½ oz. Ginger Syrup (see page 97)

2 dashes of Bittermens Hellfire Habanero Shrub

¾ oz. fresh lime juice

½ oz. agave nectar

1 lime wheel, for garnish

2 fresh sage leaves, for garnish

Place the blackberries in a highball glass and muddle them. Add crushed ice to the glass.

Place the mezcal, St-Germain, syrup, shrub, lime juice, and agave nectar in a cocktail shaker, fill it two-thirds of the way with ice, and shake until chilled.

Strain into the highball glass, garnish with the lime wheel and sage leaves, and enjoy.

BRUJERA

1½ oz. reposado tequila

½ oz. rum

2 dashes of Angostura bitters

¼ oz. agave nectar

Dash of activated charcoal

1 strip of orange peel, for garnish

Place all of the ingredients, except for the garnish, in a mixing glass, fill it two-thirds of the way with ice, and stir until chilled.

Strain over a large ice cube into a rocks glass. Express the strip of orange peel over the cocktail, use it as a garnish, and enjoy.

PINEAPPLE EXPRESS

2 oz. tequila

1 oz. Thai Chile Agave (see recipe)

1 oz. fresh lime juice

2 oz. pineapple juice

Mezcal, to mist

Pinch of kosher salt, for garnish

1 pineapple ring, for garnish

Place the tequila, agave, lime juice, and pineapple juice in a cocktail shaker, fill it two-thirds of the way with ice, and shake until chilled.

Double strain over ice into a rocks glass.

Using a spray bottle filled with mezcal, mist the cocktail. Garnish with the salt and pineapple and enjoy.

Thai Chile Agave: Place 2 oz. Thai chile peppers and 2 cups water in a saucepan and bring to a boil. Stir in 2 cups agave nectar and simmer the mixture for 1 hour. Remove the pan from heat and let the mixture cool completely. Strain before using or storing.

UNSCALPE

1½ oz. mezcal

1 oz. Kamm & Sons Islay Cask bitters

1 oz. Aperol

1 strip of orange peel, for garnish

Place the mezcal, bitters, and Aperol in a mixing glass, fill it two-thirds of the way with ice, and stir until chilled.

Strain into a goblet, garnish with the strip of orange peel, and enjoy.

PINEAPPLE EXPRESS

EL CHAVO DEL OCHO

2 oz. Tequila Ocho Blanco

½ oz. Licor 43

½ oz. fresh lime juice

¾ oz. passion fruit puree

½ oz. Thyme Syrup (see page 119)

1 egg white

1 sprig of fresh thyme, for garnish

Place all of the ingredients, except for the garnish, in a cocktail shaker, add 1 ice cube, and whip shake until chilled.

Strain into a large coupe or a wineglass, garnish with the thyme, and enjoy.

MAYA GOLD

1½ oz. Chamomile Mezcal (see recipe)

¾ oz. fino sherry

½ oz. Aperol

½ oz. Yellow Chartreuse

1 lemon twist, for garnish

Place all of the ingredients, except for the garnish, in a mixing glass, fill it two-thirds of the way with ice, and stir until chilled.

Strain into a coupe, garnish with the lemon twist, and enjoy.

Chamomile Mezcal: Place ¼ cup loose-leaf chamomile tea and 1 cup mezcal in a large mason jar and steep for 30 minutes to 1 hour, tasting the mixture every 5 minutes after the 30-minute mark to account for the varying results different mezcals will produce. When the taste is to your liking, strain and use as desired.

CULTURE VULTURE

¾ oz. Pepita Orgeat (see recipe)

1½ oz. mezcal

½ oz. añejo tequila

¾ oz. fresh lime juice

3 drops of orange blossom water

2 fresh mint leaves, plus more for garnish

14 drops of Angostura bitters

Place the orgeat, mezcal, tequila, lime juice, orange blossom water, and fresh mint in a cocktail shaker, fill it two-thirds of the way with ice, and shake until chilled.

Strain over cracked ice into a double rocks glass and top with the bitters.

Garnish with additional fresh mint and enjoy.

Pepita Orgeat: Place 1 cup pumpkin seeds in a large saucepan and toast them over medium heat. Add 2 cups water, bring to a boil, remove the pan from heat, and let the mixture cool. When it has cooled, pulse it in a blender until the mixture is a coarse meal and then strain the liquid through cheesecloth. Discard the solids, transfer the liquid to a small pot, and add an equal amount of sugar. Simmer until the sugar dissolves, stirring continually. Stir in 1½ oz. vodka and 1 teaspoon orange blossom water and let the orgeat cool completely before using or storing.

DRUNKEN RABBIT

2 oz. mezcal

1 oz. Ancho Reyes liqueur

1½ oz. pineapple juice

1½ oz. guava juice

½ oz. Cinnamon Syrup (see page 262)

Pineapple leaves, for garnish

1 orange slice, for garnish

Fresh mint, for garnish

Tajín, for garnish

Place all of the ingredients, except for the garnishes, in a blender with 1 cup of crushed ice and puree until smooth.

Pour the cocktail into a pineapple shell, tumbler, or rocks glass, garnish with pineapple leaves, an orange slice, fresh mint, and Tajín, and enjoy.

SHAKE YOUR TAMARIND

1½ oz. resposado tequila

¼ oz. mezcal

¼ oz. Campari

¾ oz. tamarind concentrate

¾ oz. Cinnamon Syrup (see page 262)

¼ oz. fresh lime juice

Fresh mint, for garnish

1 cinnamon stick, for garnish

Place all of the ingredients, except for the garnishes, in a mixing glass, fill it two-thirds of the way with ice, and stir until chilled.

Double strain into a coupe, garnish with fresh mint and the cinnamon stick, and enjoy.

RISING SUN

Salt, for the rim
1 maraschino cherry
1½ oz. tequila
⅔ oz. Yellow Chartreuse
½ oz. Lime Cordial (see page 71)
1 bar spoon sloe gin

Wet the rim of a coupe and rim it with salt. Place the cherry in the bottom of the glass.

Place the tequila, Chartreuse, and Lime Cordiall in a cocktail shaker, fill it two-thirds of the way with ice, shake until chilled, and strain into the rimmed coupe.

Top with the sloe gin, allowing it to slowly filter through the cocktail, and enjoy.

CHAMPAGNE PALOMA

¾ oz. tequila
2½ oz. pink-and-white grapefruit juice blend (1:1 ratio)
Dash of Cinnamon Syrup (see page 262)
Champagne, to top
1 grapefruit twist, for garnish

Place the tequila, juice blend, and syrup in a mixing glass, fill it two-thirds of the way with ice, and stir until chilled.

Strain into a Champagne flute, top with Champagne, garnish with the grapefruit twist, and enjoy.

EL VATO SWIZZLE

1½ oz. tequila

1 oz. fresh lime juice

¾ oz. fresh watermelon juice

¾ oz. Mexican Pepper Reduction (see recipe)

Large pinch of fresh cilantro, plus more for garnish

Dash of Peychaud's bitters

1 slice of watermelon, for garnish

Place the tequila, juices, reduction, and cilantro in a pilsner glass, add some crushed ice, and use the swizzle method (see page 9) to combine.

Top with the bitters and more crushed ice. Garnish with the slice of watermelon and additional cilantro and enjoy.

Mexican Pepper Reduction: Make sure to prepare this in a well-ventilated kitchen, as the fumes from cooking the reduction will make the air extremely peppery. Place 2 cups water, 1 dried chile de árbol, 1 ancho chile pepper, and 1 sliced jalapeño chile pepper in a saucepan, bring to a boil, and cook for 20 minutes. Strain the mixture into a mixing bowl, add 3 cups sugar, and stir until dissolved. Let the mixture cool completely before using or storing.

DESERT DAISY

1½ oz. tequila

½ oz. Amaro Averna

¾ oz. fresh lime juice

¾ oz. Orange Bell Pepper & Beet Syrup (see recipe)

4 drops of 10 Percent Saline Solution (see page 64)

10 dashes of Bittermens Hellfire Habanero Shrub

1 edible flower blossom, for garnish

Place all of the ingredients, except for the garnish, in a cocktail shaker, fill it two-thirds of the way with ice, and shake until chilled.

Strain over ice into a tumbler, garnish with the edible flower, and enjoy.

Orange Bell Pepper & Beet Syrup: Juice ½ cup chopped orange bell pepper and then strain the remaining pulp, pressing down on it to extract as much liquid as possible. Repeat with ½ cup chopped beets. Place the juices and 1 cup sugar in a saucepan and bring to a boil, stirring to dissolve the sugar. Remove the pan from heat and let the syrup cool completely before using or storing.

NAKED & FAMOUS

¾ oz. mezcal

¾ oz. Yellow Chartreuse

¾ oz. Aperol

¾ oz. fresh lime juice

Chill a coupe in the freezer.

Place all of the ingredients in a cocktail shaker, fill the shaker two-thirds of the way with ice, and shake until chilled.

Strain into the chilled coupe and enjoy.

LA DIOSA

1½ oz. tequila
¾ oz. triple sec
½ oz. fresh lime juice
1 tablespoon Pineapple Marmalade (see recipe)
½ bar spoon chili powder
1 small bunch of fresh cilantro
1 egg white
Tajín, for garnish
Edible flowers, for garnish

Place all of the ingredients, except for the egg white and garnishes, in a cocktail shaker, fill it two-thirds of the way with ice, and shake until chilled.

Strain, discard the ice, and return the mixture to the shaker. Add the egg white and dry shake for 15 seconds.

Strain into a coupe, garnish with Tajín and edible flowers, and enjoy.

Pineapple Marmalade: Peel and core 4 pineapples, dice them, and place them in a large saucepan. Add 8 cinnamon sticks, ¼ cup pure vanilla extract, 4 orange peels, 2 stemmed and seeded guajillo chile peppers, 1 cup sweet vermouth, 1 cup Lillet, and 4 cups sugar and bring to a simmer. Simmer for 5 hours, stirring occasionally, until the liquid has reduced by at least half. Remove the cinnamon sticks and chiles. Place the remaining mixture in a blender and puree until smooth. Let the marmalade cool completely before using or storing.

DIABLO OTOÑO

1 oz. tequila

1 oz. Fig Cordial (see recipe)

1 teaspoon fig liqueur

Tonic water, to top

Place all of the ingredients, except for the tonic water, in a highball glass containing three ice spheres and stir until chilled.

Top with tonic water and enjoy.

Fig Cordial: Preheat the oven to 350°F. Place 15 figs on a parchment-lined baking sheet, cover them with 3½ oz. honey, and then sprinkle 1¾ oz. walnuts around the pan. Place the pan in the oven and roast for 10 minutes. Pour the Fig Leaf Syrup (see recipe) into a saucepan and warm it over medium heat. When the figs are done, add them to the syrup and simmer for 10 minutes. Strain, stir in 1 tablespoon citric acid and 7 oz. rosé, and let the cordial cool completely before using or storing.

Fig Leaf Syrup: Place 30 fig leaves in a container and pour 3 cups Simple Syrup (see page 16) over them. Steep for 30 minutes and strain before using or storing.

PIÑA FUMADA

1¼ oz. mezcal

¾ oz. fresh lemon juice

2 teaspoons Velvet Falernum

½ oz. honey

Club soda, to top

1 pineapple leaf, for garnish

1 lemon wedge, for garnish

Place all of the ingredients, except for the club soda and garnishes, in a cocktail shaker, fill it two-thirds of the way with ice, and shake until chilled.

Strain over crushed ice into a highball glass and top with club soda.

Add more crushed ice, garnish with the pineapple leaf and lemon wedge, and enjoy.

LOST IN THE RAIN IN JUÁREZ

1 oz. mezcal

¾ oz. Aperol

⅞ oz. fresh lime juice

½ oz. Demerara Syrup (see page 65)

1¼ oz. pineapple juice

3 dashes of absinthe

1 egg white

1 dehydrated pineapple chunk, for garnish

Place all of the ingredients, except for the garnish, in a cocktail shaker and dry shake for 15 seconds.

Add ice and shake until chilled.

Double strain into a coupe, garnish with the chunk of dehydrated pineapple, and enjoy.

MEZCAL SURVIVOR

1¾ oz. mezcal

⅞ oz. Cocchi Americano

¾ oz. Lime Syrup (see recipe)

⅞ oz. fresh lemon juice

Absinthe, to mist

3 maraschino cherries, for garnish

Place the mezcal, Cocchi Americano, syrup, and lemon juice in a cocktail shaker, fill it two-thirds of the way with ice, and shake until chilled.

Strain into a cocktail glass and mist the cocktail with absinthe. If desired, light the absinthe on fire. Garnish with the maraschino cherries, skewered on a toothpick, and enjoy.

Lime Syrup: Prepare a batch of Demerara Syrup (see page 65). While the syrup is still warm, stir in the zest of 3 limes and 1 cup fresh lime juice. Steep for 15 minutes, strain, and let the syrup cool completely before using or storing.

CANTARITOS

2 oz. reposado tequila

1½ oz. fresh orange juice

¾ oz. fresh pink grapefruit juice

½ oz. fresh lime juice

2 pinches of kosher salt

2 oz. pink grapefruit soda

1 lime wedge, for garnish

Add the ingredients, except for the garnish, to a Collins glass filled with ice.

Gently stir to combine, garnish with the lime wedge, and enjoy.

FIRE WALK WITH ME

½ oz. fresh lime juice

½ oz. Orgeat (see page 103)

2 slices of jalapeño chile pepper

2 oz. reposado tequila

½ oz. Velvet Falernum

1 strip orange peel, for garnish

Place the lime juice, Orgeat, and jalapeño in a cocktail shaker and muddle.

Add ice, the tequila, and falernum and shake until chilled.

Strain into a coupe, garnish with the strip of orange peel, and enjoy.

MÁMÙ VIDA

¾ oz. Szechuan & Chipotle Honey (see recipe)

¾ oz. fresh lemon juice

2 oz. mezcal

1 Szechuan flower, for garnish

Pinch of flaky sea salt, for garnish

Place the honey, lemon juice, and mezcal in a cocktail shaker, fill it two-thirds of the way with ice, and shake until chilled.

Strain over ice into a double rocks glass, garnish with the Szechuan flower and pinch of salt, and enjoy.

Szechuan & Chipotle Honey: Place ½ oz. Szechuan peppercorns in a saucepan and toast until they are fragrant, shaking the pan frequently. Add 4½ oz. torn chipotle meco chile peppers and 2 cups water and bring to a boil. Reduce the heat and simmer for 5 minutes. Strain, add 2 cups honey, and stir until combined. Remove the pan from heat and let the mixture cool completely before using or storing.

DONS OF SOUL

1⅔ oz. tequila
1 oz. fresh tomato, chopped
⅔ oz. paprika
2 bar spoons fresh lime juice
2 bar spoons fresh lemon juice
1 bar spoon agave nectar
¼ teaspoon chili powder
Pinch of pink pepper
Dash of Bob's Coriander Bitters
1 strip of lime peel, for garnish

Place all of the ingredients, except for the garnish, in a blender and pulse until combined.

Strain the mixture into a mixing glass, fill it two-thirds of the way with ice, and stir until chilled.

Strain into a cocktail glass, garnish with the strip of lime peel, and enjoy.

JALISCO SOUR

1 oz. tequila
1 oz. pisco
¾ oz. fresh lime juice
¾ oz. Simple Syrup (see page 16)
3 dashes of Angostura bitters, for garnish

Place the tequila, pisco, lime juice, and syrup in a cocktail shaker, fill it two-thirds of the way with crushed ice, and shake until chilled.

Strain into a coupe, garnish with the bitters, and enjoy.

FLOR DE JALISCO

TRUE ROMANCE

1½ oz. mezcal
1 oz. Yellow Chartreuse
¾ oz. Amaro Averna
1 lime twist, for garnish
Pinch of sea salt, for garnish

Place the mezcal, Chartreuse, and amaro in a rocks glass containing one large ice cube and stir until chilled.

Garnish with the lime twist and sea salt and enjoy.

FLOR DE JALISCO

1½ oz. reposado tequila
½ oz. mezcal
½ oz. strawberry jam
½ oz. agave nectar
½ oz. fresh lime juice
Dash of Black Lava Solution (see recipe)
3 dashes of Bittermens Hellfire Habanero Shrub
2 pineapple leaves, for garnish
1 lime wheel, for garnish
1 marigold blossom, for garnish

Place all of the ingredients, except for the garnishes, in a cocktail shaker, fill it two-thirds of the way with ice, and shake until chilled.

Strain over ice into a rocks glass and garnish with the pineapple leaves, lime wheel, and marigold blossom.

Black Lava Solution: Place ½ cup water and ¼ cup black lava salt in a saucepan and bring to a boil, stirring until the salt has dissolved. Remove the pan from heat and let the solution cool completely before using or storing.

L & N

1½ oz. Cincoro Tequila Reposado
¾ oz. Honey & Basil Syrup (see recipe)
2 dashes of Angostura bitters
Bittermens Xocolatl Mole Bitters, to taste
1 strip of orange peel, for garnish

Place all of the ingredients, except for the garnish, in a cocktail shaker, fill it two-thirds of the way with ice, and shake until chilled.

Strain the cocktail into a coupe, garnish with the strip of orange peel, and enjoy.

Honey & Basil Syrup: Place 1 cup honey and 1 cup water in a saucepan and bring to a simmer, stirring until the honey has emulsified. Remove the pan from heat, add 2 handfuls of fresh basil leaves, and let the syrup cool completely. Strain before using or storing.

PAN

1 oz. tequila
⅓ oz. dry vermouth
⅓ oz. Lemongrass Syrup (see recipe)
⅔ oz. pear puree
1 sprig of fresh dill, for garnish
1 piece of fresh ginger, for garnish

Place the tequila, vermouth, syrup, and puree in a cocktail shaker, fill it two-thirds of the way with ice, and shake until chilled.

Strain into a goblet, garnish with the dill and ginger, and enjoy.

Lemongrass Syrup: Place 1 cup water, 1 cup sugar, and 3 peeled and bruised lemongrass stalks in a saucepan and bring to a boil, stirring to dissolve the sugar. Remove the pan from heat, let the syrup cool completely, and strain before using or storing.

PAN

GUERA

1½ oz. tequila

1 oz. grapefruit juice

¾ oz. fresh lime juice

¼ oz. Aperol

¼ oz. St-Germain

¼ oz. Thai Pepper Shrub (see recipe)

Fever-Tree Bitter Lemon Soda, to top

1 grapefruit wheel, for garnish

1 lime wheel, for garnish

Place all of the ingredients, except for the soda and garnishes, in a Collins glass, add ice, and stir until chilled.

Top with soda, garnish with the grapefruit wheel and lime wheel, and enjoy.

Thai Pepper Shrub: Place 4 chopped Thai chile peppers, ¼ cup cane vinegar, and ¼ cup cane sugar in a saucepan and bring to a boil, stirring to dissolve the sugar. Cook for 5 minutes, remove the pan from heat, and let the shrub cool completely. Strain before using or storing.

LA MULA

1½ oz. Olmeca Altos Plata Tequila

½ oz. Domaine de Canton

1 oz. fresh lime juice

4 slices of jalapeño chile pepper, plus more for garnish

4 oz. ginger beer

Place all of the ingredients, except for the ginger beer and the garnish, in a cocktail shaker, fill it two-thirds of the way with ice, and shake until chilled.

Double strain over ice into a rocks glass and top with the ginger beer.

Garnish with additional jalapeño and enjoy.

SUNDAY MORNING COMING DOWN

1⅜ oz. tequila

½ oz. dry vermouth

⅜ oz. Aperol

1 teaspoon agave nectar

5 drops of chile pepper extract

1 strip of orange peel, for garnish

Place all of the ingredients, except for the garnish, in a mixing glass and fill it two-thirds of the way with ice. Using another, empty mixing glass, pour the cocktail back and forth between the glasses until combined.

Strain over two ice cubes into a cocktail glass. Express the strip of orange peel over the cocktail, use it as a garnish, and enjoy.

EL NACIONAL

1 oz. Del Maguey Vida Mezcal

1 oz. Campari

½ oz. Luxardo Amaro Abano

½ oz. dry vermouth

3 dashes of Bittermens Xocolatl Mole Bitters

Spritz of Ardbeg 5-Year Islay Scotch Whisky, to top

1 lemon twist, for garnish

Place all of the ingredients, except for the Scotch and garnish, in a mixing glass, fill it two-thirds of the way with ice, and stir until chilled.

Strain the cocktail into a coupe and spritz it with the Ardbeg.

Garnish with the lemon twist and enjoy.

VIOLET SKIES

¾ oz. Butterfly Pea Flower–Infused Mezcal (see recipe)

½ oz. Hood River Distillers Lewis and Clark's Lookout Northwest Gin

½ oz. Ventura Spirits Strawberry Brandy

¼ oz. Kalani Coconut Rum Liqueur

¼ oz. Rothman & Winter Crème de Violette

½ oz. fresh lemon juice

2 dashes of Scrappy's Grapefruit Bitters

1 edible flower, for garnish

Chill a coupe in the freezer.

Place all of the ingredients, except for the garnish, in a cocktail shaker and dry shake for 10 seconds. Add ice and shake vigorously until chilled.

Double strain into the chilled coupe, garnish with the edible flower, and enjoy.

Butterfly Pea Flower–Infused Mezcal: Place 2 tablespoons dried butterfly pea flowers and a 750 ml bottle of mezcal in a large mason jar, shake vigorously, and let the mixture steep for 3 hours. Strain before using or storing.

TEQUILA TROPIC

1 teaspoon caster (superfine) sugar

4 oz. orange juice

Juice of ½ lemon

Juice of ½ lime

2 oz. tequila

1 orange wheel, for garnish

Place the sugar, juices, and tequila in a cocktail shaker, fill it two-thirds of the way with ice, and shake until chilled.

Strain over ice into a rocks glass, garnish with the orange wheel, and enjoy.

EL DIABLO

1½ oz. tequila
1 oz. crème de cassis
Juice of 1 lime
Ginger beer, to top
2 to 3 raspberries, for garnish
2 to 3 blackberries, for garnish
1 lime slice, for garnish

Place the tequila, liqueur, and lime juice in a cocktail shaker, fill it two-thirds of the way with ice, and shake until chilled.

Strain over ice into a tumbler and top with ginger beer.

Garnish with the raspberries, blackberries, and lime slice and enjoy.

PEPINO

1 oz. Simple Syrup (see page 16)
3 fresh cilantro leaves
3 cucumber slices
2 oz. tequila
1 oz. orange liqueur
1 oz. pineapple juice
Juice of ½ lime
1 lime wedge, for garnish
1 pineapple slice, for garnish

Place the syrup, cilantro, and cucumber slices in a cocktail shaker and muddle.

Add the tequila, orange liqueur, juices, and ice and shake until chilled.

Strain over ice into a highball glass, garnish with the lime wedge and pineapple slice, and enjoy.

HOME IS WHERE THE HEAT IS

Black lava salt, for the rim

Cumin, for the rim

1½ oz. Spicy Mezcal (see recipe)

¼ oz. Giffard Banane du Brésil liqueur

½ oz. fresh lime juice

½ oz. Manzanilla sherry

¾ oz. Tamarind Syrup (see recipe)

1 slice of dehydrated jalapeño chile pepper, for garnish

Place lava salt and cumin in a dish and stir to combine. Wet the rim of a double rocks glass and rim it with the mixture.

Place the remaining ingredients, except for the garnish, in a cocktail shaker, fill it two-thirds of the way with ice, and shake until chilled.

Strain over ice into the rimmed glass, garnish with the dehydrated slice of jalapeño, and enjoy.

Spicy Mezcal: Place 2 to 3 sliced jalapeño chile peppers in a 750 ml bottle of mezcal and let the mixture steep for 24 hours. Strain before using or storing.

Tamarind Syrup: Place ¼ cup tamarind pulp, 1 cup water, and 1 cup sugar in a saucepan and bring to a simmer, stirring to dissolve the sugar and incorporate the tamarind. Remove the pan from heat and let the syrup cool completely. Strain before using or storing.

PINEAPPLE LEAP

1¼ oz. tequila

2 oz. pineapple juice

1 oz. fresh lemon juice

¼ oz. grenadine

Place all of the ingredients in a cocktail shaker, fill it two-thirds of the way with ice, and shake until chilled.

Strain over crushed ice into a Collins glass and enjoy.

SHADYSIDE FIZZ

1 egg white

¾ oz. fresh lime juice

1 oz. tequila

1 oz. Angostura bitters, plus 3 drops for garnish

¾ oz. Simple Syrup (see page 16)

Sprite, to top

Place the egg white and lime juice in a cocktail shaker and dry shake for 10 to 15 seconds.

Add ice, the tequila, bitters, and syrup, and shake until chilled.

Strain over ice into a Collins glass and top with Sprite.

Garnish with the additional bitters and enjoy.

BERLIN IN '77

1 oz. mezcal

1 oz. tequila

1 oz. orange juice

½ oz. fresh lemon juice

½ oz. Cinnamon Syrup (see page 262)

Dash of Angostura bitters

1 orange wheel, for garnish

Place the mezcal, tequila, juices, and syrup in a cocktail shaker, fill it two-thirds of the way with ice, and shake until chilled.

Strain into a double rocks glass and top with the bitters.

Garnish with the orange wheel and enjoy.

LOVEJOY

1 oz. tequila

¾ oz. mezcal

¾ oz. fresh lime juice

¾ oz. Watermelon & Prickly Pear Shrub (see recipe)

6 drops of 10 Percent Saline Solution (see page 64)

1 grapefruit slice, for garnish

Place the tequila, mezcal, lime juice, shrub, and saline solution in a cocktail shaker, fill it two-thirds of the way with ice, and shake until chilled.

Strain over pebble ice into a highball glass, garnish with the grapefruit slice, and enjoy.

Watermelon & Prickly Pear Shrub: Place ½ cup apple cider vinegar, ½ cup sugar, ¼ cup watermelon cubes, and 2 tablespoons prickly pear puree in a saucepan and bring to a boil, mashing the watermelon with a wooden spoon and stirring to dissolve the sugar. Cook for 5 minutes, remove the pan from heat, and let the shrub cool completely. Strain before using or storing.

PALOMA

PALOMA

Salt, for the rim

2 oz. tequila

1 oz. fresh grapefruit juice

½ oz. fresh lime juice

½ oz. Simple Syrup (see page 16)

2 oz. seltzer water

1 grapefruit slice, for garnish

Wet the rim of a Collins glass and rim half of it with salt.

Place the tequila, juices, and syrup in a cocktail shaker, add 1 to 2 ice cubes, and whip shake until chilled.

Pour the cocktail into the rimmed glass, top with the seltzer, and add more ice. Garnish with the grapefruit slice and enjoy.

THE BRAVE

1 oz. Del Maguey Chichicapa Mezcal

1 oz. Tequila Cabeza

½ oz. Amaro Averna

¼ oz. curaçao

3 mists of Angostura bitters

1 torched strip of orange peel, for garnish

Place the mezcal, tequila, amaro, and curaçao in a wineglass, add ice, and stir until chilled.

Mist the glass above the cocktail with the bitters, garnish with the torched strip of orange peel, and enjoy.

HOT MESS

½ oz. Serrano Grenadine (see recipe)

⅓ oz. Cholula hot sauce

1¾ oz. reposado tequila

¾ oz. fresh lemon juice

1 lemon wheel, for garnish

Place the grenadine, hot sauce, tequila, and lemon juice in a cocktail shaker, fill it two-thirds of the way with ice, and shake until chilled.

Strain over ice into a rocks glass, garnish with the lemon wheel, and enjoy.

Serrano Grenadine: Place 1 cup pomegranate juice and 2 diced serrano chile peppers in a saucepan over medium heat and cook until the mixture is syrupy. Remove from heat and let the grenadine cool. Strain before using or storing.

GINGER PALOMA

2 oz. tequila

1 oz. fresh ruby red grapefruit juice

½ oz. fresh lime juice

¼ oz. Ginger Syrup (see page 97)

2½ oz. seltzer water

Pinch of kosher salt

1 grapefruit wedge, for garnish

Chill a Collins glass in the freezer.

Place the tequila, juices, and syrup in a cocktail shaker, add 2 tablespoons of crushed ice, and shake until chilled.

Strain over ice into the chilled Collins glass and top with the seltzer water and salt.

Garnish with the grapefruit wedge and enjoy.

TORONHA

2 oz. tequila

½ oz. orange liqueur

2 oz. grapefruit juice

Dash of orange juice

Dash of grenadine

1 cup ice

1 strawberry, for garnish

Place the tequila, liqueur, juices, grenadine, and ice in a blender and puree until smooth.

Pour into a mason jar, garnish with the strawberry, and enjoy.

CARDS ON THE TABLE

2 dashes of Cardamom Tincture (see recipe)

2 oz. tequila

¾ oz. fresh lemon juice

¾ oz. Simple Syrup (see page 16)

Cracked black pepper, for garnish

Place the tincture, tequila, lemon juice, and syrup in a cocktail shaker, fill it two-thirds of the way with ice, and shake until chilled.

Strain into a coupe, garnish with the cracked black pepper, and enjoy.

Cardamom Tincture: Place ½ cup high-proof vodka and 1 tablespoon lightly crushed cardamom pods in a mason jar and muddle. Cover the mixture and store it in a cool, dark place for 3 to 5 days, shaking every day. When the flavor is to your liking, strain and use as desired.

THIRD PLAYER

¾ oz. mezcal

½ oz. cachaça

½ oz. Cardamom & Cinnamon Maple Syrup (see recipe)

½ oz. fresh lime juice

¼ oz. pisco

¼ oz. apricot liqueur

¼ oz. Ancho Reyes

½ oz. Orgeat **(see page 103)**

¼ oz. Falernum

2 dashes of Bittermens Xocolatl Mole Bitters

Pinch of kosher salt

Cinnamon sticks, crushed, for garnish

Place all of the ingredients, except for the garnish, in a cocktail shaker, fill it two-thirds of the way with ice, and shake until chilled.

Strain over crushed ice into a rocks glass, garnish with crushed cinnamon sticks, and enjoy.

Cardamom & Cinnamon Maple Syrup: Place 2 cinnamon sticks and 3 black cardamom pods in a skillet and toast over medium heat until fragrant, shaking the pan frequently. Remove the aromatics from the pan and set them aside. Place 1 cup maple syrup and ½ cup water in a saucepan and bring to a simmer. Add the toasted spices and simmer for 5 minutes. Remove the pan from heat and let the mixture cool for 1 hour. Strain before using or storing.

HAY ZEUS

THE HATCHBACK

1½ oz. tequila
¾ oz. Campari
½ oz. fresh lime juice
½ oz. fresh ruby red grapefruit juice
½ oz. Simple Syrup (see page 16)
Topo Chico, to top
1 grapefruit slice, for garnish

Place all of the ingredients, except for the Topo Chico and garnish, in a cocktail shaker, fill it two-thirds of the way with ice, and shake until chilled.

Strain over ice into a mason jar and top with Top Chico.

Garnish with the grapefruit slice and enjoy.

HAY ZEUS

½ oz. tequila
½ oz. fresh lime juice
1¾ oz. Zeus Juice Cordial (see recipe)
Cornflower leaves, for garnish

Place all of the ingredients, except for the garnish, in a cocktail shaker, fill it two-thirds of the way with ice, and shake until chilled.

Strain over a block of ice into a ceramic bowl or cup, garnish with the cornflower leaves, and enjoy.

Zeus Juice Cordial: Place ⅜ oz. hay, 5¼ oz. celery juice, and 3½ oz. caster (superfine) sugar in a blender and pulse until combined. Strain through cheesecloth and stir in ⅞ oz. Simple Syrup (see page 16), 1 cup mezcal, 3½ oz. Gik blue wine, ½ oz. 10 Percent Saline Solution (see page 64), and 2 drops of MSK Toasted Coconut Flavour Drops. Use as desired.

YOU HAD ME AT HIBISCUS

½ oz. Hibiscus Syrup (see page 20)
¾ oz. fresh lemon juice
¼ oz. Luxardo maraschino liqueur
1½ oz. reposado tequila
Dried hibiscus blossoms, for garnish

Place the syrup, lemon juice, liqueur, and tequila in a cocktail shaker, fill it two-thirds of the way with ice, and shake until chilled.

Double strain into a coupe, garnish with dried hibiscus, and enjoy.

BLESSING OF AGAVE

1½ oz. tequila
½ oz. Aperol
¾ oz. fresh grapefruit juice
¼ oz. fresh lime juice
½ oz. agave nectar
1 egg white
1 strip of grapefruit peel, for garnish

Place the tequila, Aperol, juices, agave nectar, and egg white in a cocktail shaker and dry shake for 10 to 15 seconds.

Add ice and shake until chilled.

Double strain into a coupe, garnish with the strip of grapefruit peel, and enjoy.

PALOMA REYNA

¾ oz. Grapefruit & Thyme Cordial (see recipe)

1½ oz. tequila

½ oz. fresh lime juice

Topo Chico, to top

1 strip of orange peel, for garnish

1 sprig of fresh thyme, for garnish

Place the cordial, tequila, and lime juice in a cocktail shaker, fill it two-thirds of the way with ice, and shake until chilled.

Strain over ice into a Collins glass and top with Topo Chico.

Garnish with the strip of orange peel and fresh thyme and enjoy.

Grapefruit & Thyme Cordial: Peel 2 ruby red grapefruits, discard the peels, and squeeze the juice into a small saucepan. Add the juice of 2 large lemons, a handful of fresh thyme, and 2 tablespoons sugar and cook over low heat, stirring to dissolve the sugar. Once the sugar has dissolved, allow the mixture to simmer for 30 minutes before removing the cordial from heat and letting it cool completely. Strain before using or storing.

THE FIFTH ELEMENT

Citrus Salt (see recipe), for the rim

2 oz. tequila

2 oz. Avocado Mix (see recipe)

¾ oz. fresh lime juice

½ oz. agave nectar

1 egg white

1 dehydrated lemon slice, for garnish

Wet the rim of a coupe and rim it with the Citrus Salt.

Place all of the remaining ingredients, except for the garnish, in a cocktail shaker, fill it two-thirds of the way with ice, and shake until chilled.

Strain into the coupe, garnish with the dehydrated lemon slice, and enjoy.

Citrus Salt: Place the zest of 2 lemons, zest of 2 limes, and ½ cup kosher salt in a mixing bowl, stir to combine, and use as desired.

Avocado Mix: Place the flesh of 1½ avocados, 1 lb. diced pineapple, and ¾ lb. fresh cilantro in a blender, puree until smooth, and use as desired.

SILK STOCKING

2 oz. tequila

1 oz. heavy cream

1 oz. crème de cacao

1 teaspoon Chambord

Chill a cocktail glass in the freezer.

Place all of the ingredients in a cocktail shaker, fill it two-thirds of the way with ice, and shake until chilled.

Strain into the chilled cocktail glass and enjoy.

THUNDER GUN EXPRESS

4 orange wedges
2 dashes of cardamom bitters
1 oz. Honey Syrup (see page 64)
¾ oz. Amaro Montenegro
1 oz. Del Maguey Vida Mezcal

Place the orange wedges in a cocktail shaker and muddle.

Add the bitters, syrup, amaro, mezcal, and ice and shake until chilled.

Strain over ice into a rocks glass and enjoy.

THE ONLY WORD

¾ oz. tequila
¾ oz. fresh lime juice
¾ oz. Green Chartreuse
¾ oz. Luxardo maraschino liqueur
¼ oz. mezcal
Dash of celery bitters
1 lime wheel, for garnish

Place the tequila, lime juice, Chartreuse, Luxardo, mezcal, and bitters in a cocktail shaker, fill it two-thirds of the way with ice, and shake until chilled.

Strain into a coupe, garnish with the lime wheel, and enjoy.

DARK WINGS

1 oz. tequila

1 oz. blackberry liqueur

Juice of 1 lime

2 oz. ginger beer

Fresh blackberries, for garnish

Place the tequila, liqueur, and lime juice in a cocktail shaker, fill it two-thirds of the way with ice, and shake until chilled.

Strain over ice into a highball glass and top with the ginger beer.

Garnish with blackberries and enjoy.

AMY JO JOHNSON

1 strawberry, plus 1 for garnish

3 fresh basil leaves, plus 1 for garnish

1½ oz. mezcal

¾ oz. fresh lime juice

¾ oz. Simple Syrup (see page 16)

1 teaspoon Ume Shrub (see recipe)

Place the strawberry and fresh basil in a cocktail shaker and muddle.

Add the mezcal, lime juice, syrup, shrub, and ice and shake until chilled.

Strain over a large ice cube into a rocks glass, garnish with an additional strawberry and fresh basil, and enjoy.

Ume Shrub: Place 1 cup umeshu and ½ cup balsamic vinegar in a small saucepan and bring to a boil over medium heat. Cook until the shrub has reduced slightly and remove the pan from heat. Let the shrub cool completely before using or storing.

MR. KOTTER

MR. KOTTER

2 oz. Tapatio Tequila

½ oz. Pierre Ferrand Dry Curaçao

1 oz. fresh lime juice

¼ oz. agave nectar

1 orange wedge, for garnish

Place all of the ingredients, except for the garnish, in a cocktail shaker, fill it two-thirds of the way with ice, and shake until chilled.

Double strain over a Hibiscus Ice Cube (see recipe) into a rocks glass, garnish with the orange wedge, and enjoy.

Hibiscus Ice Cubes: Place 8 cups water, 1 cup dried hibiscus blossoms, and 1 orange peel in a saucepan and bring to a boil. Remove the pan from heat and let the mixture steep for 3 hours. Strain, pour the strained liquid into ice molds, and freeze until the ice cubes are solid.

BURNING IN EFFIGY

2 oz. tequila

½ oz. Strega

½ oz. fresh lemon juice

¼ oz. Ancho Reyes

½ oz. crème de cacao

Mexican chocolate, grated, for garnish

1 strip of lemon peel, for garnish

Place the tequila, Strega, lemon juice, Ancho Reyes, and crème de cacao in a cocktail shaker, fill it two-thirds of the way with ice, and shake until chilled.

Double strain into a coupe, garnish with grated chocolate and the strip of lemon peel, and enjoy.

SPICY MARGARITA

Tajín, for the rim
2 oz. silver tequila
½ oz. Cointreau
1 oz. fresh lime juice
½ oz. Blistered Jalapeño Syrup (see recipe)
3 dashes of 10 Percent Saline Solution (see page 64)
1 lime wedge, for garnish

Wet the rim of a double rocks glass and rim half of it with Tajín.

Place all of the ingredients, except for the garnish, in a cocktail shaker, fill it two-thirds of the way with ice, and shake until chilled.

Pour the cocktail into the rimmed glass and add more ice if desired. Garnish with the lime wedge and enjoy.

Blistered Jalapeño Syrup: Warm a comal or large cast-iron skillet over medium heat. Add 6 stemmed and sliced jalapeño chile peppers and cook until they are lightly charred, turning them occasionally. Place the jalapeños in a blender, add 2 cups water and 2 cups caster (superfine) sugar, and puree on high for 30 seconds. Strain the syrup into a mason jar and use as desired.

DESERT SPOON

2 oz. reposado tequila
½ oz. Cointreau
2 oz. ruby red grapefruit juice
1 oz. fresh lime juice
½ oz. agave nectar
1 sprig of fresh rosemary, for garnish

Place the tequila, Cointreau, juices, and agave nectar in a cocktail shaker, fill it two-thirds of the way with ice, and shake until chilled.

Strain into a coupe, garnish with the fresh rosemary, and enjoy.

ANTICUADO

1½ oz. reposado tequila
½ lime, cut into thirds
4 dashes of Angostura bitters
1 oz. fresh orange juice
½ oz. agave nectar
1 torched lime twist, for garnish

Place the tequila, lime, and bitters in a cocktail shaker and muddle.

Add the orange juice, agave nectar, and ice and shake until chilled.

Double strain into a coupe, garnish with the torched lime twist, and enjoy.

TIA MIA

1 oz. mezcal
1 oz. Jamaican rum
¾ oz. fresh lime juice
½ oz. Orgeat (see page 103)
½ oz. curaçao
1 lime wheel, for garnish
1 orchid blossom, for garnish
Fresh mint, for garnish

Place the mezcal, rum, lime juice, Orgeat, and curaçao in a cocktail shaker, fill it two-thirds of the way with ice, and shake until chilled.

Strain over crushed ice into a rocks glass, garnish with the lime wheel, orchid blossom, and fresh mint, and enjoy.

BAJA LEMONADE

1 sprig of fresh rosemary

1 oz. tequila

Splash of coconut rum

2 oz. lemonade

1 lemon wheel, for garnish

Place the fresh rosemary, tequila, and coconut rum in a cocktail shaker, fill it two-thirds of the way with ice, and shake until chilled.

Strain over ice into a highball glass and top with the lemonade.

Garnish with the lemon wheel and enjoy.

FUEGO DE COLIMA

1¾ oz. tequila

¾ oz. Ginger & Lemongrass Cordial (see recipe)

2 teaspoons spiced rum

½ oz. Simple Syrup (see page 16)

Place all of the ingredients in a cocktail shaker, fill it two-thirds of the way with ice, and shake until chilled.

Strain into a rocks glass and enjoy.

Ginger & Lemongrass Cordial: Peel and slice 1 large piece of fresh ginger and place it in a saucepan. Add 1 bruised lemongrass stalk, 2 cups water, and 1½ cups sugar and bring to a simmer, stirring occasionally, for 20 minutes. Remove the cordial from heat and let it cool completely. Strain before using or storing.

LA CONQUISTADOR

Spicy salt, for the rim

½ oz. reposado tequila

½ oz. silver tequila

½ oz. white crème de cacao

½ oz. fresh lime juice

1 teaspoon agave nectar

5 to 7 dashes of Fee Brothers Aztec Chocolate Bitters

1 lime wedge, for garnish

Wet the rim of a rocks glass and rim it with spicy salt.

Place the tequilas, crème de cacao, lime juice, agave nectar, and bitters in a cocktail shaker, fill it two-thirds of the way with ice, and shake until chilled.

Strain over a large ice cube into the rimmed rocks glass, garnish with the lime wedge, and enjoy.

MIDNIGHT MARAUDER

1 oz. mezcal

1 oz. Bonal Gentiane-Quina

1 oz. Cynar

Dash of Bittermens Xocolatl Mole Bitters

Chill a Nick & Nora glass in the freezer.

Place all of the ingredients in a mixing glass, fill it two-thirds of the way with ice, and stir until chilled.

Strain into the chilled Nick & Nora glass and enjoy.

TEQUILA SUNRISE

1 oz. tequila

Dash of fresh lemon juice

Orange juice, to top

Splash of grenadine

1 maraschino cherry, for garnish

1 orange slice, for garnish

Fill a Daiquiri glass with ice, add the tequila and lemon juice, and stir until chilled.

Top with orange juice, add the grenadine, and let it filter down through the cocktail.

Garnish with the maraschino cherry and orange slice and enjoy.

SMOKE ON THE BEACH

1 oz. mezcal

1 oz. tequila

1 oz. fresh lime juice

1 oz. pineapple juice

½ oz. agave nectar

1 strip of orange peel, for garnish

Place the mezcal, tequila, juices, and agave nectar in a cocktail shaker, fill it two-thirds of the way with ice, and shake until chilled.

Double strain into a coupe and express the strip of orange peel over the drink.

Garnish the cocktail with the strip of orange peel and enjoy.

TEQUILA SUNRISE

OAXACAN BOTTLE ROCKET

Handful of fresh mint, plus more for garnish

¾ oz. Del Maguey Vida Mezcal

¾ oz. Smith & Cross Traditional Jamaica Rum

1 oz. fresh lime juice

¾ oz. Thai Chile & Basil Syrup (see recipe)

½ oz. Velvet Falernum

½ oz. orange juice

Peychaud's bitters, to top

Place the fresh mint at the bottom of a Collins glass and fill the glass with pebble ice.

Fill the glass with the remaining ingredients, except for the bitters, and top with more pebble ice.

Top with bitters until you see a nice red layer on the top of the drink. Garnish with additional fresh mint and enjoy.

Thai Chile & Basil Syrup: Add 3 diced Thai chile peppers and a handful of fresh Thai basil to 2 cups Simple Syrup (see page 16) and let the mixture steep in the refrigerator for 2 days. Strain before using or storing.

BLOODY MARIA

Cracked black pepper, for the rim, plus more to taste
2 oz. tequila
½ oz. olive brine
Juice of 1 lime wedge
2 dashes of horseradish
Tomato juice, to top
3 drops of Worcestershire sauce
3 dashes of hot sauce
2 dashes of celery salt
1 celery stalk, for garnish
1 lemon wedge, for garnish

Wet the rim of a pint glass or mason jar and rim it with cracked black pepper.

Add ice, the tequila, olive brine, lime juice, and horseradish, top with tomato juice, and stir to combine.

Add the Worcestershire sauce, hot sauce, and celery salt, season with black pepper, and stir until chilled.

Garnish with the celery stalk and lemon wedge and enjoy.

NO SAY

1¾ oz. mezcal
¾ oz. Aperol
½ oz. coconut liqueur
1 oz. fresh lime juice
½ oz. pineapple juice
¾ oz. Lemongrass Syrup (see page 160)
1 makrut lime leaf, for garnish

Place the mezcal, Aperol, liqueur, juices, and syrup in a cocktail shaker, fill it two-thirds of the way with ice, and shake until chilled.

Strain over ice into a rocks glass, garnish with the makrut lime leaf, and enjoy.

CROSSEYED & PAINLESS

⅛ oz. Herbsaint
¾ oz. sloe gin
¾ oz. tequila
¾ oz. curaçao
¾ oz. Lillet Rouge
Dash of Angostura bitters
1 lemon twist, for garnish

Rinse a coupe with the Herbsaint and discard the excess.

Place the gin, tequila, curaçao, Lillet, and bitters in a mixing glass, fill it two-thirds of the way with ice, and stir until chilled.

Strain into the rinsed coupe, garnish with the lemon twist, and enjoy.

SHE'S A RAINBOW

2 oz. tequila

1 oz. Midori

5 oz. white grapefruit juice

1 grapefruit slice, for garnish

Place the ingredients in a cocktail shaker, fill it two-thirds of the way with ice, and shake until chilled.

Strain over ice into a highball glass and garnish with the slice of grapefruit.

COFFEE IN CHIHUAHUA

1 cinnamon stick

2 oz. Coffee-Infused Reposado Tequila (see recipe)

1 bar spoon agave nectar

3 dashes of Angostura bitters

Light one end of the cinnamon stick on fire, place it under an upside-down rocks glass, and let it smolder so that smoke accumulates in the glass.

Place the tequila, agave nectar, and bitters in a mixing glass, fill it two-thirds of the way with ice, and stir until chilled.

Discard the cinnamon stick, add ice to the smoked glass, strain the drink over it, and enjoy.

Coffee-Infused Reposado Tequila: Place 2 tablespoons ground coffee in a filter, tie it closed, and place it in 6 oz. tequila. Steep for 4 hours, remove the coffee, and strain before using or storing.

SHE'S A RAINBOW

LAVAGAVE

1½ oz. tequila
½ oz. mezcal
¾ oz. Lavender Agave (see recipe)
½ oz. grapefruit juice
½ oz. fresh lime juice
¾ oz. egg whites
Dash of Bittercube Cherry Bark Vanilla Bitters
Dried lavender buds, grated, for garnish

Place all of the ingredients, except for the garnish, in a cocktail shaker, fill it two-thirds of the way with ice, and shake until chilled.

Strain, discard the ice in the shaker, return the cocktail to the shaker, and dry shake for 15 seconds.

Pour the drink into a coupe and garnish with grated lavender buds.

Lavender Agave: Place 1 teaspoon dried lavender buds in a piece of cheesecloth and use kitchen twine to turn it into a sachet. Place 4 cups agave nectar in a saucepan and bring it to a boil. Remove the pan from heat, add the lavender sachet, and let the mixture steep for 2 hours. Remove the sachet before using or storing.

MANDARIN KISS

2 oz. Maker's Mark Bourbon

2 tablespoons Mandarin Puree (see recipe)

Splash of soda water

1 orange slice, for garnish

Place the bourbon and puree in a cocktail shaker, fill it two-thirds of the way with ice, and shake until chilled.

Pour the contents of the shaker into a tumbler and top with the soda water.

Garnish with the orange slice and enjoy.

Mandarin Puree: Peel, segment, and, if necessary, seed 4 mandarin oranges. Place the oranges in a blender with 1 tablespoon sugar and 1 teaspoon fresh lemon juice and pulse until chopped. Puree until smooth, taste, and add more sugar or lemon juice as desired. Use immediately or store in the refrigerator.

WASHINGTON APPLE

1 oz. Crown Royal

1 oz. apple vodka

1 oz. cranberry juice

7UP, to top

Place the Crown Royal, apple vodka, and cranberry juice in a cocktail shaker, fill it two-thirds of the way with ice, and shake until chilled.

Strain over ice into a rocks glass, top with 7UP, and enjoy.

WHISKEY SUNSET

2 oz. bourbon

2 oz. white wine

1 oz. lemonade

Dash of Simple Syrup (see page 16)

3 oz. ginger ale

1 lemon wheel, for garnish

Fill a mason jar with ice, add the bourbon, white wine, lemonade, and syrup, and stir until chilled.

Top with the ginger ale, garnish with the lemon wheel, and enjoy.

BROWN DERBY

2 oz. maple whiskey

2 oz. grapefruit juice

½ oz. honey

1 grapefruit slice, for garnish

Place the maple whiskey, grapefruit juice, and honey in a cocktail shaker, fill it two-thirds of the way with ice, and shake until chilled.

Strain over ice into a highball glass, garnish with the grapefruit slice, and enjoy.

QUEEN OF THE DAMNED

1½ oz. rye whiskey
½ oz. Cognac
¾ oz. fresh lime juice
½ oz. Hibiscus Cordial (see recipe)
¼ oz. Amaro Nonino
Fresh mint, for garnish
1 lime wheel, for garnish

Place all of the ingredients, except for the garnishes, in a cocktail shaker, fill it two-thirds of the way with ice, and shake until chilled.

Strain over ice into a Collins glass, garnish with fresh mint and the lime wheel, and enjoy.

Hibiscus Cordial: Bring 4 cups water to a boil in a saucepan and turn off the heat. Add 1 oz. loose-leaf hibiscus tea and steep for 10 minutes. Add 1 oz. peeled and sliced fresh ginger, 2 cinnamon sticks, 6 allspice berries, 2 whole cloves, the zest of 1 lemon, and 3 cups sugar and bring the mixture to a gentle simmer. Cook for 15 minutes, stirring to dissolve the sugar. Remove the pan from heat and let the mixture steep overnight. Strain before using or storing.

ROB ROY

2 oz. Scotch whisky
1 oz. sweet vermouth
2 drops of Angostura bitters
1 maraschino cherry

Place the Scotch, sweet vermouth, and bitters in a mixing glass, fill it two-thirds of the way with ice, and stir until chilled.

Place the maraschino cherry in a cocktail glass, strain the cocktail over it, and enjoy.

QUEEN OF THE DAMNED

RENEGADE LEMONADE

1 oz. Simple Syrup **(see page 16)**

1½ oz. fresh lemon juice

1 oz. whiskey

4 oz. water

Fresh mint, for garnish

2 lemon wheels, for garnish

Place the syrup, lemon juice, whiskey, and water in a cocktail shaker, fill it two-thirds of the way with ice, and shake until chilled.

Strain over ice into a Collins glass, garnish with fresh mint and the lemon wheels, and enjoy.

SWEET TEA PUNCH

1 lemon wedge

2 fresh mint leaves

1 oz. bourbon

4 oz. sweet tea

2 lemon wheels, for garnish

Place the lemon wedge, fresh mint, and bourbon in a mixing glass and muddle. Add ice and stir until chilled.

Strain over ice into a highball glass.

Top with the sweet tea, garnish with the lemon wheels, and enjoy.

TATAMI

2 (3- to 4-inch) lemongrass stalks

½ oz. Suntory Yamazaki 12-Year-Old Whisky

1 teaspoon dark crème de cacao

1 oz. pineapple juice

⅓ oz. Simple Syrup (see page 16)

1 teaspoon apricot brandy

1 teaspoon fresh lemon juice

1 lemon twist, for garnish

Dip the lemongrass stalks into the bottle of whisky, ignite them with a lighter, and shake them to extinguish the flames. Set the lemongrass aside.

Place the whisky and crème de cacao in a mixing glass, stir to combine, and set the mixture aside.

Place the pineapple juice, syrup, apricot brandy, and lemon juice in a cocktail shaker, fill it two-thirds of the way with ice, and shake until chilled.

Double strain into a cocktail glass and top with the whisky mixture.

Add the torched lemongrass stalks, garnish with the lemon twist, and enjoy.

MISH MASH

2 oz. bourbon

1 oz. triple sec

1 oz. Simple Syrup (see page 16)

Splash of grenadine

Fill a highball glass with ice, add the bourbon, triple sec, and syrup, and stir until chilled.

Top with the grenadine and enjoy.

QUARTER TANK OF GASOLINE

QUARTER TANK OF GASOLINE

2 oz. Nelson's Green Brier Tennessee Whiskey

1 oz. Sassafras Syrup (see recipe)

½ oz. fresh lemon juice

Fresh mint, for garnish

Place all of the ingredients, except for the ganrish, in a cocktail shaker, fill it two-thirds of the way with ice, and shake until chilled.

Strain the cocktail over ice into a rocks glass, garnish with fresh mint, and enjoy.

Sassafras Syrup: Place 3 sprigs of fresh mint, the zest of 2 lemons, and 1½ cups Simple Syrup (see page 16) in a large mason jar and muddle. Add 1½ cups sassafras tea concentrate, shake to combine, and chill the syrup in the refrigerator overnight before straining and using.

RAINY SEASON

1⅓ oz. Suntory Hibiki 12-Year-Old Whisky

1 teaspoon fresh lemon juice

4 cucumber slices

½ teaspoon umeboshi

⅓ oz. Simple Syrup (see page 16)

Fresh mint, for garnish

Place the whisky, lemon juice, and cucumber slices in a blender and puree until smooth.

Add the umeboshi and syrup and puree until well incorporated.

Add small handfuls of ice and puree until the mixture has the consistency of a smoothie.

Spoon into a Nick & Nora glass, garnish with fresh mint, and enjoy.

GREEN BREEZE

4 fresh mint leaves, plus more for garnish
Splash of white crème de menthe
1 oz. Suntory Hakushu 12-Year-Old Whisky
Splash of tonic water
Soda water, to top

Place the fresh mint and crème de menthe in a highball glass, muddle with a bar spoon, and strain to discard the liqueur.

Add a large ice sphere to the glass. Add the whisky and tonic water and top with soda water.

Garnish with the additional fresh mint and enjoy.

MANHATTAN

2 oz. WhistlePig Straight Rye Whiskey
⅔ oz. sweet vermouth
2 drops of orange bitters
1 Luxardo maraschino cherry

Place the whiskey, sweet vermouth, and bitters in a mixing glass, fill it two-thirds of the way with ice, and stir until chilled.

Place the maraschino cherry in a cocktail glass, strain the cocktail over it, and enjoy.

MAPLE MARRIAGE

1⅔ oz. Japanese whisky

⅓ oz. maple syrup

⅓ oz. yuzu juice

1 egg white

8 drops of ginger bitters

1 strip of yuzu peel, for garnish

Place the whisky, maple syrup, yuzu juice, and egg white in a cocktail shaker, fill it two-thirds of the way with ice, and shake until frothy.

Strain into a coupe, top with the bitters, arranging them in a circular pattern, and use a toothpick to connect the droplets.

Garnish with the strip of yuzu peel and enjoy.

AROMATIC CHICHIBU

1⅓ oz. Japanese whisky

⅔ oz. Bénédictine

⅓ oz. sweet vermouth

⅓ oz. black currant puree

1 teaspoon Fernet-Branca

Chill a wineglass in the freezer.

Place all of the ingredients in a mixing glass, fill it two-thirds of the way with ice, and stir until chilled.

Strain into the chilled wineglass and enjoy.

HIJINKS

1½ oz. Glenmorangie X Scotch Whisky
¾ oz. Lustau Fino Sherry
¾ oz. Chamomile Syrup (see recipe)
½ oz. fresh lemon juice
1 dehydrated lemon wheel, for garnish

Place all of the ingredients, except for the garnish, in a cocktail shaker, fill it two-thirds of the way with ice, and shake until chilled.

Strain the cocktail into a coupe, garnish with the dehydrated lemon wheel, and enjoy.

Chamomile Syrup: Prepare Simple Syrup (see page 16) and add 1 tablespoon chamomile blossoms or 2 bags of chamomile tea after the sugar has dissolved. Remove the pan from heat, let the syrup cool, and strain before using or storing.

WHISKEY SOUR

2 oz. whiskey
1 oz. fresh lemon juice
Splash of water
Pinch of caster (superfine) sugar
1 maraschino cherry, for garnish

Fill a rocks glass with ice, add the whiskey, lemon juice, water, and sugar, and stir until chilled.

Garnish with the maraschino cherry and enjoy.

HIJINKS

WHISKEY & COKE

1 oz. whiskey

3 oz. Coca-Cola

Juice of 1 lime

Fill a highball glass with ice, add the whiskey and cola, and stir until chilled.

Add the lime juice, gently stir, and enjoy.

REDNECK LEMONADE

1 oz. whiskey

3 oz. hard lemonade

Fill a highball glass with ice and add the whiskey and hard lemonade.

Stir until chilled and enjoy.

BOURBON SWEET TEA

1 oz. bourbon

2 oz. sweet tea

½ oz. fresh lemon juice

Fill a rocks glass with ice, add the bourbon and sweet tea, and stir until chilled.

Top with the lemon juice and enjoy.

BROOKLYN IS IN THE USA

1½ oz. rye whiskey
1½ oz. dry vermouth
½ teaspoon Luxardo maraschino liqueur
½ teaspoon Ramazzotti

Place all the ingredients in a mixing glass, fill it two-thirds of the way with ice, and stir until chilled.

Strain into a coupe and enjoy.

IRISH COFFEE

1 oz. Jameson Irish Whiskey
4 oz. hot coffee
1 oz. Baileys Irish Cream
Sugar, to taste

Place the whiskey, coffee, and Irish cream in a mug and stir.

Add sugar, stir again, and enjoy.

WAKEUP CIDER

1 oz. whiskey
2 oz. apple cider
1 oz. sparkling cider

Fill a rocks glass with ice, add the whiskey and still apple cider, and stir until chilled.

Top with the sparkling cider, gently stir, and enjoy.

OLD FASHIONED

James Bond embedded the Martini in the public consciousness, and the Old Fashioned also owes its current popularity to a figment of someone's imagination. As the go-to drink for the stylish, and extremely thirsty, Don Draper on the lauded TV show *Mad Men*, the Old Fashioned lost the extraneous elements—club soda is just one—that had been appended to it over the years, returned to its roots, and became the quintessential whiskey cocktail.

The key to mastering the Old Fashioned is exploring the space within the drink's narrow parameters in order to find a spot that's entirely your own. Try out different bitters, or use a mixture, such as a few drops of Angostura bitters and Regans' Orange Bitters. Remove the cherry and instead add a bit of the juice from a jar of Luxardo maraschino cherries or Griottines before adding the whiskey. Add the strip of orange peel with the sugar and muddle it, or switch it out for a piece of orange zest. When you really start to drill down into the elements of this simple cocktail, the possibilities are endless.

1 sugar cube
2 drops of Angostura bitters
Splash of water
2 oz. Woodford Reserve Bourbon
1 strip of orange peel, for garnish
1 Luxardo maraschino cherry, for garnish

Place the sugar cube, bitters, and water in a rocks glass and muddle.

Add ice and the bourbon and stir until chilled.

Garnish with the strip of orange peel and maraschino cherry and enjoy.

BLACKBERRY SAGE JULEP

2 blackberries, plus 1 for garnish

1 sprig of fresh sage, plus more for garnish

½ oz. Demerara Syrup (see page 65)

2 oz. Four Roses Bourbon

Place the blackberries in a cocktail shaker and muddle.

Add ice, the sage, syrup, and bourbon and gently shake for 5 seconds.

Strain into a rocks glass and fill the glass with crushed ice.

Garnish with the additional blackberry and sage and enjoy.

MADAME ROUGE

2 oz. single-malt whisky

1 oz. Amaro Averna

2 oz. dry sparkling wine

Chill a Champagne flute in the freezer.

Place the whisky and amaro in a mixing glass, fill it two-thirds of the way with ice, and stir until chilled.

Strain into the chilled Champagne flute, top with the sparkling wine, and enjoy.

MANHATTAN IN THE SPRING

2 oz. bourbon

½ oz. Lillet

½ oz. sweet vermouth

Chill a cocktail glass in the freezer.

Place all of the ingredients in a mixing glass, fill it two-thirds of the way with ice, and stir until chilled.

Strain into the chilled cocktail glass and enjoy.

THE BASTILLE CELEBRATION

2 oz. single-malt whisky

Splash of St-Germain

Champagne, to top

Chill a Champagne flute in the freezer.

Place the whisky and St-Germain in the chilled Champagne flute, top with the Champagne, and enjoy.

THE LAFAYETTE

5 fresh mint leaves, slapped

1¾ oz. bourbon

¾ oz. fresh lemon juice

1¼ oz. grapefruit juice

¾ oz. mandarin liqueur

Place all of the ingredients in a cocktail shaker, fill it two-thirds of the way with ice, and shake until chilled.

Strain over ice into a highball glass and enjoy.

THE YEAR OF THE FRENCHMAN

2 oz. single-malt whisky

½ oz. agave nectar

¾ oz. fresh lime juice

3 dashes of celery bitters

1 teaspoon Sorel hibiscus liqueur

Chill a coupe in the freezer.

Place the whisky, agave nectar, lime juice, and bitters in a cocktail shaker, fill it two-thirds of the way with ice, and shake until chilled.

Strain into the chilled coupe, top with the hibiscus liqueur, and enjoy.

WHALEN SMASH

½ lemon, cut into thirds

4 fresh mint leaves

3 oz. bourbon

1 oz. ginger beer

1 lemon wheel, for garnish

Squeeze the juice from the lemon wedges into a rocks glass. Add the spent lemon wedges and the mint and muddle.

Add ice and the bourbon and top with the ginger beer.

Gently stir until chilled, garnish with the lemon wheel, and enjoy.

14 JULLIET

Juice of 4 lime wedges

2 oz. single-malt whisky

¼ oz. Fig Syrup (see recipe)

Ginger beer, to top

Fill a cocktail glass with ice, add the lime juice, whisky, and syrup, and stir until chilled.

Top with ginger beer and enjoy.

Fig Syrup: Prepare Simple Syrup (see page 16) in a medium saucepan. While the syrup is boiling, add 4 halved figs and mash them with a wooden spoon. Remove the pan from heat and let the syrup cool completely. Strain before using or storing.

THE LAST CALL

2 oz. single-malt whisky

1 oz. Sorel hibiscus liqueur

Chill a coupe in the freezer.

Place the ingredients in a cocktail shaker, fill it two-thirds of the way with ice, and shake until chilled.

Strain into the chilled coupe and enjoy.

MINT JULEP

This drink is permanently associated with Kentucky, both due to the Kentucky Derby, where it became the official beverage in 1938, and because of the bourbon that the state is renowned for producing. This is the version preferred by legendary Kentucky senator Henry Clay, who helped popularize the cocktail when he brought it to Washington, DC in the nineteenth century.

In a proper Mint Julep, you want to recognize the priority established in the cocktail's name, and give the mint most of your attention so that you can extract as much of the mint's aroma as possible, since the Julep is a drink that is meant to charm the nose as much as the taste buds. If you are still struggling to lock in the taste, try stirring the cocktail after adding the bourbon. It's not traditional, as purists feel the additional agitation will dilute the cocktail too much, but it just may add an element that you will find extremely pleasing.

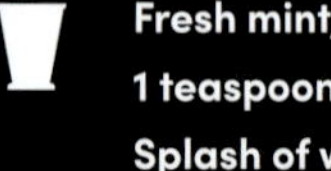

Fresh mint, torn, plus more for garnish
1 teaspoon confectioners' sugar
Splash of water
2 oz. Maker's Mark Bourbon
2 dashes of bitters

Place the fresh mint, confectioners' sugar, and water in a Julep cup and muddle.

Add crushed ice and the bourbon and gently stir until chilled.

Top with more crushed ice and the bitters.

Garnish with additional fresh mint and enjoy.

BLACK POINT

1½ oz. Johnnie Walker Double Black Scotch Whisky

¼ oz. orange bitters

¼ oz. Yellow Chartreuse

1 teaspoon Grand Marnier

1 dehydrated orange wheel, for garnish

Place the whisky, bitters, Chartreuse, and Grand Marnier in a mixing glass, fill it two-thirds of the way with ice, and stir until chilled.

Strain into a Nick & Nora glass, garnish with the dehydrated orange wheel, and enjoy.

MR. SMOOTH

2 oz. bourbon

¼ oz. Cognac

¼ oz. Cynar

¼ oz. Demerara Syrup (see page 65)

2 dashes of Angostura bitters

1 strip of orange peel, for garnish

Place all of the ingredients, except for the garnish, in a mixing glass, fill it two-thirds of the way with ice, and stir until chilled.

Strain the cocktail into a coupe, garnish with the strip of orange peel, and enjoy.

MR. SMOOTH

MOONFLOWER

1½ oz. Chivas Regal 12-Year-Old Scotch Whisky
2 oz. cold-brew coffee
½ oz. Dubonnet Rouge
5 drops of absinthe
½ oz. Perrier

Place the whisky, coffee, Dubonnet Rouge, and absinthe in a mixing glass, fill it two-thirds of the way with ice, and stir until chilled.

Strain over ice into a Collins glass and top with the Perrier.

Gently stir to combine and enjoy.

NIGHT BIRD

1¾ oz. single-malt Scotch whisky
1 bar spoon gum syrup
5 dashes of crème de violette
2 drops of Dr. Adam Elmegirab's Teapot Bitters

Chill a cocktail glass in the freezer.

Place all of the ingredients in a mixing glass, fill it two-thirds of the way with ice, and stir until chilled.

Strain into the chilled cocktail glass and enjoy.

BOURBON BALL MILKSHAKE

4 scoops of vanilla ice cream

2 oz. Buffalo Trace Bourbon Cream

2 oz. chocolate fudge

Chocolate syrup, to taste

Dollop of whipped cream, for garnish

Candied pecans, for garnish

Chill a Hurricane glass or pint glass in the freezer.

Place the ice cream, bourbon cream, and fudge in a blender and puree until smooth.

Drizzle chocolate syrup along the walls of the chilled glass and pour the ice cream mixture into the glass.

Top with additional chocolate syrup, the whipped cream, and candied pecans and enjoy.

CHARBONNEAU WAY

Absinthe, to mist

2 oz. rye whiskey

½ oz. fresh lemon juice

½ oz. maple syrup

½ oz. Suze

1 sprig of fresh thyme, for garnish

Mist a coupe with absinthe.

Place the whiskey, lemon juice, maple syrup, and Suze in a cocktail shaker, fill it two-thirds of the way with ice, and shake until chilled.

Strain into the coupe, garnish with the fresh thyme, and enjoy.

SCOTCH & SALT

4 drops of Smoked Salt Tincture (see recipe)

1½ oz. Scotch whisky

¾ oz. Cocchi Americano

¾ oz. Cocchi Vermouth di Torino

½ oz. white grapefruit juice

1 strip of orange peel, for garnish

Place the tincture, Scotch, Cocchi Americano, vermouth, and grapefruit juice in a cocktail shaker, fill it two-thirds of the way with ice, and shake until chilled.

Strain over a large ice cube into a double rocks glass, garnish with the strip of orange peel, and enjoy.

Smoked Salt Tincture: In a small bowl, dissolve 2 teaspoons hickory-smoked salt in 4 oz. water. Use as desired.

STREETCAR NAMED DESIRE

1½ oz. bourbon

¾ oz. Mint & Lemon Verbena Syrup (see recipe)

¾ oz. fresh lemon juice

4 dashes of Angostura bitters

Fresh mint, for garnish

Place the bourbon, syrup, and lemon juice in a cocktail shaker, fill it two-thirds of the way with ice, and shake until chilled.

Strain over ice into a rocks glass and top with the bitters.

Garnish with fresh mint and enjoy.

Mint & Lemon Verbena Syrup: Prepare Simple Syrup (see page 16) and add 3 sprigs of fresh mint and 2 sprigs of fresh lemon verbena as it comes to a boil. Remove the pan from heat, steep until the syrup has cooled, and strain before using or storing.

ARNAUD'S SPECIAL COCKTAIL

2 oz. Scotch whisky

1 oz. Dubonnet Rouge

3 dashes of orange bitters

1 orange twist, for garnish

Place the Scotch, Dubonnet Rouge, and bitters in a cocktail shaker, fill it two-thirds of the way with ice, and shake until chilled.

Strain into a rocks glass, garnish with the orange twist, and enjoy.

ABERDEEN

½ oz. Lapsang Souchong Syrup (see recipe)

2 dashes of Jack Rudy Aromatic Bitters

2 oz. Scotch whisky

1 strip of orange peel

Fill a rocks glass with ice, add the syrup, bitters, and Scotch, and stir until chilled.

Express the strip of orange peel over the drink, drop it into the glass, and enjoy.

Lapsang Souchong Syrup: Prepare Simple Syrup (see page 16) and add 2 bags of lapsang souchong tea as it comes to a boil. Remove the pan from heat, steep until the syrup has cooled, and remove the tea bags before using or storing.

PENICILLIN

PENICILLIN

¾ oz. Honey & Ginger Syrup (see recipe)

2 oz. blended Scotch whisky

¾ oz. fresh lemon juice

¼ oz. smoky Islay single-malt Scotch whisky (Laphroaig or Lagavulin recommended), to float

Place the syrup, blended Scotch, and lemon juice in a cocktail shaker, fill it two-thirds of the way with ice, and shake until chilled.

Strain over ice into a rocks glass. Float the single-malt Scotch on top by pouring it slowly over the back of a spoon and enjoy.

Honey & Ginger Syrup: Place 1 cup water, 1 cup honey, and a chopped 2-inch piece of fresh ginger in a saucepan and bring to a boil. Cook for 4 minutes, remove the pan from heat, and let the syrup cool completely. Strain before using or storing.

PARIS BETWEEN THE WARS

1 oz. smoky Scotch whisky

¾ oz. Campari

¾ oz. fresh lemon juice

½ oz. Honey Syrup (see page 64)

3 oz. dry pear cider

1 strip of grapefruit peel, for garnish

Place the Scotch, Campari, lemon juice, and syrup in a cocktail shaker, fill it two-thirds of the way with ice, and shake until chilled.

Strain over ice into a Collins glass and top with the cider.

Express the strip of grapefruit peel over the drink, garnish the cocktail with it, and enjoy.

THE BIG CHIEF

2 oz. bourbon

½ oz. Amaro Nonino

½ oz. Punt e Mes

1 torched strip of orange peel, for garnish

Place the bourbon, amaro, and Punt e Mes in a mixing glass, fill it two-thirds of the way with ice, and stir until chilled.

Strain into a Nick & Nora glass and express the torched strip of orange peel over the drink.

Garnish the cocktail with the torched strip of orange peel and enjoy.

BOULEVARDIER

2 oz. rye whiskey

1 oz. Campari

½ oz. Antica Forumula Sweet Vermouth

1 lemon twist, for garnish

Place the whiskey, Campari, and sweet vermouth in a mixing glass, fill it two-thirds of the way with ice, and stir until chilled.

Strain into a coupe, garnish with the lemon twist, and enjoy.

LITTLE ITALY

2 oz. Rittenhouse Rye

½ oz. Cynar

¾ oz. Martini & Rossi Sweet Vermouth

2 Luxardo maraschino cherries, for garnish

Chill a cocktail glass in the freezer.

Place the rye, Cynar, and vermouth in a mixing glass, fill it two-thirds of the way with ice, and stir until chilled.

Strain into the chilled cocktail glass, garnish with the maraschino cherries, and enjoy.

SFORZANDO

1 oz. rye whiskey

¾ oz. Del Maguey Chichicapa Mezcal

½ oz. Bénédictine

½ oz. Dolin Blanc Vermouth

2 dashes of Bittermens Xocolatl Mole Bitters

1 orange twist, for garnish

Place the rye, mezcal, Bénédictine, vermouth, and bitters in a mixing glass, fill it two-thirds of the way with ice, and stir until chilled.

Strain into a cocktail glass, garnish with the orange twist, and enjoy.

NEW YORK SOUR

2 oz. Famous Grouse Smoky Black Scotch Whisky

¾ oz. Simple Syrup (see page 16)

¾ oz. fresh lemon juice

¼ oz. dry red wine

1 lemon wheel, for garnish

1 brandied cherry, for garnish

Place the Scotch, syrup, and lemon juice in a cocktail shaker, fill it two-thirds of the way with ice, and shake until chilled.

Strain over ice into a rocks glass and float the red wine on top, pouring it over the back of a spoon.

Garnish with the lemon wheel and brandied cherry and enjoy.

TRINIDAD SOUR

1½ oz. Angostura bitters

½ oz. rye whiskey

¾ oz. fresh lemon juice

1 oz. Orgeat (see page 103)

Place all of the ingredients in a cocktail shaker, fill it two-thirds of the way with ice, and shake until chilled.

Strain into a coupe and enjoy.

NEW YORK SOUR

FORTH & CLYDE

FORTH & CLYDE

Honey, as needed

Red pepper flakes, to taste

1 oz. Maker's Mark Bourbon

1 oz. Hendrick's Gin

1 oz. St-Germain

1 oz. fresh lime juice

Chill a cocktail glass in the freezer.

Pour a nickel-sized quantity of honey into a cocktail shaker.

Add red pepper flakes and the remaining ingredients and stir until the honey has dissolved.

Add as much ice as you can fit into the shaker and shake for 18 seconds.

Strain the cocktail into the chilled cocktail glass and enjoy.

BLOOD, LUST & DIAMONDS

2 oz. rye whiskey

¾ oz. Bonal Gentiane-Quina

½ oz. Cognac

Dash of Angostura bitters

Dash of Peychaud's bitters

Dash of amaretto

1 Luxardo maraschino cherry, for garnish

Place the whiskey, Bonal Gentiane-Quina, Cognac, bitters, and amaretto in a mixing glass, fill it two-thirds of the way with ice, and stir until chilled.

Strain into a coupe, garnish with the maraschino cherry, and enjoy.

VIEUX CARRÉ

¾ oz. rye whiskey

¾ oz. Cognac

¾ oz. sweet vermouth

1 bar spoon Bénédictine

Splash of Peychaud's bitters

Dash of Angostura bitters

1 lemon twist, for garnish

Place the whiskey, Cognac, sweet vermouth, Bénédictine, and bitters in a mixing glass, fill it two-thirds of the way with ice, and stir until chilled.

Strain over ice into a rocks glass, garnish with the lemon twist, and enjoy.

WHISKEY BUSINESS

1 oz. rye whiskey

1 oz. Ancho Reyes

½ oz. fresh lemon juice

½ oz. Cinnamon Syrup (see page 262)

1 ancho chile powder–dusted lemon wheel, for garnish

Place the rye, Ancho Reyes, lemon juice, and syrup in a cocktail shaker, fill it two-thirds of the way with ice, and shake until chilled.

Strain over a large ice cube into a rocks glass, garnish with the chile-dusted lemon wheel, and enjoy.

MARGOT TENENBAUM

2 oz. bourbon

¾ oz. fresh lemon juice

½ oz. Honey Syrup (see page 64)

½ oz. Zucca Rabarbaro

Place all of the ingredients in a cocktail shaker, fill it two-thirds of the way with ice, and shake until chilled.

Strain into a coupe and enjoy.

DON LOCKWOOD

Dash of Angostura bitters

2 dashes of chocolate bitters

⅜ oz. maple syrup

1 oz. Islay Scotch whisky

1 oz. bourbon

1 long orange twist, for garnish

Fill a rocks glass with ice, add the bitters, maple syrup, Scotch, and bourbon, and stir until chilled.

Garnish with the orange twist and enjoy.

BANKER'S PUNCH

3 dashes of Angostura bitters
¾ oz. fresh lime juice
¾ oz. raspberry cordial
¾ oz. port
¾ oz. Redbreast 12-Year-Old Irish Whiskey
¾ oz. Jamaican Rum Blend (see recipe)
Freshly grated nutmeg, for garnish

Place the bitters, lime juice, cordial, port, whiskey, and rum blend in a cocktail shaker, fill it two-thirds of the way with ice, and shake until chilled.

Strain over a few large ice cubes into a rocks glass, garnish with nutmeg, and enjoy.

Jamaican Rum Blend: Combine equal parts of Wray & Nephew, Appleton Estate Signature, and Hamilton Jamaican Black rums.

PSYCHO KILLER

¾ oz. Cacao Nib–Infused Campari (see recipe)
2 dashes of absinthe
½ oz. crème de cacao
½ oz. Giffard Banane du Brésil liqueur
2 oz. Redbreast 12-Year-Old Irish Whiskey

Place all of the ingredients in a mixing glass, fill it two-thirds of the way with ice, and stir until chilled.

Strain into a cocktail glass and enjoy.

Cacao Nib–Infused Campari: Place 1 cup Campari and 1 tablespoon cacao nibs in a mason jar, shake until combined, and steep for 1 hour, shaking the jar occasionally. Strain before using or storing.

TENNESSEE BELLINI

1 oz. Gentleman Jack Tennessee Whiskey

1 oz. peach puree

Champagne, to top

Place the whiskey and peach puree in a Champagne flute and stir to combine.

Top with Champagne and enjoy.

THE SCOTCH CRINGE

1 egg

¾ oz. fresh lime juice

2 oz. Scotch whisky

¾ oz. Simple Syrup (see page 16)

2 watermelon cubes

Place the egg and lime juice in a cocktail shaker and shake for 10 to 15 seconds.

Add the remaining ingredients, muddle the watermelon, and shake until chilled.

Strain over ice into a Collins glass and enjoy.

THE MARATHON MAN

1 oz. FEW Bourbon

¾ oz. Kahlúa

2 teaspoons Orgeat (see page 103)

¾ oz. Frangelico

¾ oz. Mozart Dark Chocolate Liqueur

1 tablespoon peanut butter

1½ oz. whole milk

1 miniature Snickers bar, plus 1 for garnish

Place all of the ingredients, except for the garnish, in a blender along with two large ice cubes and pulse until there are fine bubbles throughout and the ice has been thoroughly incorporated.

Pour over ice into a rocks glass, garnish with an additional miniature Snickers bar, and enjoy.

ANALOGUE

1 oz. Four Roses Bourbon

1½ oz. dark rum

½ oz. Velvet Falernum

¼ oz. Domaine de Canton ginger liqueur

¼ oz. St. Elizabeth Allspice Dram

3 dashes of Angostura bitters

1 lemon twist, for garnish

Place the bourbon, dark rum, falernum, Domaine de Canton, allspice dram, and bitters in a mixing glass, fill it two-thirds of the way with ice, and stir until chilled.

Strain over a large ice cube into a rocks glass, garnish with the lemon twist, and enjoy.

THE MARATHON MAN

NIGHT TRIPPER

1¾ oz. bourbon

¾ oz. Luxardo Amaro Abano

¼ oz. Strega

2 dashes of Peychaud's bitters

1 strip of orange peel, for garnish

Place the bourbon, amaro, Strega, and bitters in a mixing glass, fill it two-thirds of the way with ice, and stir until chilled.

Strain over ice into a brandy snifter, garnish with the strip of orange peel, and enjoy.

DORIAN GRAY

½ oz. Rosemary-Infused Maple Syrup (see recipe)

1½ oz. Scotch whisky

¾ oz. pear liqueur

¾ oz. fresh lemon juice

½ oz. dry vermouth

2 dashes of Angostura bitters

Freshly grated nutmeg, for garnish

Place the maple syrup, Scotch, liqueur, lemon juice, dry vermouth, and bitters in a cocktail shaker, fill it two-thirds of the way with ice, and shake until chilled.

Strain into a coupe, garnish with nutmeg, and enjoy.

Rosemary-Infused Maple Syrup: Place 1 sprig of fresh rosemary and 1½ oz. maple syrup in a microwave-safe bowl and microwave on high for 30 seconds. Let the syrup cool and remove the rosemary before using or storing.

SCREEN DOOR SLAM

Absinthe, to rinse

1 oz. Vanilla-Infused Aperol (see recipe)

2 oz. Maker's Mark Bourbon

¼ oz. Honey Syrup (see page 64)

1 strip of orange peel, for garnish

Rinse a rocks glass with absinthe and discard any excess.

Place the Aperol, bourbon, and syrup in a mixing glass, fill it two-thirds of the way with ice, and stir until chilled.

Strain over a large ice cube into the rocks glass, garnish with the strip of orange peel, and enjoy.

Vanilla-Infused Aperol: Split 1 vanilla bean down the middle, place it in a bottle of Aperol, and steep for at least 3 days. Strain the mixture when you are ready to use it or leave the bean inside the bottle if you prefer a stronger vanilla flavor.

BIG IRON

2 oz. New York Distilling Co. Mister Katz's Rock & Rye

Dash of Angostura bitters

Dash of orange bitters

1 orange or lemon twist, for garnish

Place the whiskey and bitters in a mixing glass, fill it two-thirds of the way with ice, and stir until chilled.

Strain over ice into a rocks glass, garnish with the orange twist, and enjoy.

THE COUNTRY LAWYER

THE COUNTRY LAWYER

1½ oz. Four Roses Bourbon

½ oz. Zucca Rabarbaro

½ oz. Dolin Dry Vermouth

¼ oz. Bénédictine

Dash of chocolate bitters

1 strip of orange peel, for garnish

Place all of the ingredients, except for the garnish, in a mixing glass, fill it two-thirds of the way with ice, and stir until chilled.

Strain into a cocktail glass, garnish with the strip of orange peel, and enjoy.

PICTURING WILD FIELDS

1 bar spoon Orgeat (see page 103)

¼ oz. St-Germain

½ oz. Suze

¾ oz. pisco

1½ oz. single-malt Scotch whisky

1 lemon twist, for garnish

Chill a Nick & Nora glass in the freezer.

Place the Orgeat, St-Germain, Suze, pisco, and Scotch in a mixing glass, fill it two-thirds of the way with ice, and stir until chilled.

Strain into the chilled Nick & Nora glass, garnish with the lemon twist, and enjoy.

INNUENDO

¾ oz. Peach Syrup (see recipe)

2 oz. Corsair Triple Smoke Whiskey

1 oz. iced tea

¼ oz. fresh lemon juice

1 strip of lemon peel, for garnish

Place the syrup, whiskey, iced tea, and lemon juice in a cocktail shaker, fill it two-thirds of the way with ice, and shake until chilled.

Strain over ice into a rocks glass, garnish with the strip of lemon peel, and enjoy.

Peach Syrup: Place 1 cup water and 1 cup sugar in a saucepan and bring to a boil. Add 1 sliced peach to the saucepan, stir, and reduce the heat so that the syrup simmers. Cook for 25 minutes, remove from heat, and let the syrup cool. Strain before using or storing.

WHISKEY SLING

4 oz. Tennessee whiskey

1 oz. fresh lemon juice

1½ oz. Simple Syrup (see page 16)

2 dashes of orange bitters

1 lemon wheel, for garnish

Place the whiskey, lemon juice, syrup, and bitters in a cocktail shaker, fill it two-thirds of the way with ice, and shake until chilled.

Strain over ice into a rocks glass, garnish with the lemon wheel, and enjoy.

TENNESSEE MULE

1 oz. Jack Daniel's Old No. 7 Tennessee Whiskey
½ oz. fresh lime juice
3 oz. ginger beer
1 lime wheel, for garnish
Fresh mint, for garnish

Fill a copper mug with ice, add the whiskey, lime juice, and ginger beer, and stir until chilled.

Garnish with the lime wheel and fresh mint and enjoy.

SELECT & STAVE

1 oz. Tennessee whiskey
¾ oz. sweet vermouth
¾ oz. Cherry Heering
1 oz. fresh orange juice
1 strip of orange peel, for garnish

Place the whiskey, sweet vermouth, cherry liqueur, and orange juice in a cocktail shaker, fill it two-thirds of the way with ice, and shake until chilled.

Strain into a cocktail glass, garnish with the strip of orange peel, and enjoy.

IRISH BREEZE

¾ oz. Teeling Irish Whiskey

1½ oz. freshly brewed espresso

⅔ oz. Hibiscus Syrup (see page 20)

1½ oz. heavy cream, lightly whipped

Dehydrated strawberry powder, for garnish

Place the whiskey, espresso, and syrup in a mixing glass, fill it two-thirds of the way with ice, and stir until chilled.

Strain into a cocktail glass and float the lightly whipped cream on top by gently pouring it over the back of a spoon.

Garnish with dehydrated strawberry powder and enjoy.

OLD HAUNT

¾ oz. rye whiskey

¾ oz. Cognac

¾ oz. Noilly Prat Rouge vermouth

¼ teaspoon Bénédictine

2 dashes of Peychaud's bitters

2 dashes of Angostura bitters

Fill a rocks glass with ice, add all of the ingredients, stir until chilled, and enjoy.

IRISH BREEZE

DEAL BREAKER

Absinthe, to rinse

Dash of rhubarb bitters, to rinse

2 oz. Corsair Quinoa Whiskey

½ oz. honey

2 dashes of Peychaud's bitters

1 orange slice, for garnish

Rinse a cocktail glass with absinthe and the rhubarb bitters and discard any excess.

Place the whiskey, honey, and bitters in a mixing glass, fill it two-thirds of the way with ice, and stir until chilled.

Strain into the cocktail glass, garnish with the orange slice, and enjoy.

DARK SIDE

2 oz. bourbon

¾ oz. Simple Syrup (see page 16)

1 oz. Bonal Gentiane-Quina

¾ oz. fresh lime juice

7 dashes of Regans' Orange Bitters No. 6

1 lime wheel, for garnish

Place the whiskey, syrup, Bonal Gentiane-Quina, lime juice, and bitters in a cocktail shaker, fill it two-thirds of the way with ice, and shake until chilled.

Double strain over ice into a Collins glass, garnish with the lime wheel, and enjoy.

SOUTHERN CHARM

3 watermelon cubes

2 oz. Four Roses Bourbon

1 oz. Monin Watermelon Syrup

½ oz. PAMA Pomegranate Liqueur

4 to 5 drops of Bittermens Hopped Grapefruit Bitters

½ oz. fresh lime juice

8 fresh mint leaves, plus more for garnish

3 half-moons of cucumber

1 oz. Mr. Q. Cumber Sparkling Cucumber Beverage

Place the watermelon cubes in a cocktail shaker, muddle, and pour out the juice.

Add ice, the bourbon, watermelon syrup, pomegranate liqueur, bitters, lime juice, and fresh mint, and shake until chilled.

Double strain over crushed ice into a rocks glass.

Place the cucumber and cucumber soda in a dry cocktail shaker, muddle, and shake until combined.

Double strain to top the mixture in the rocks glass, garnish with additional fresh mint, and enjoy.

BUFFALO BOWTIE

1½ oz. Buffalo Trace Bourbon

1 oz. Peach Syrup (see page 248)

Ginger ale, to top

1 lime twist, for garnish

Fill a highball glass with ice, add the bourbon and syrup, and stir until chilled.

Top with ginger ale, garnish with the lime twist, and enjoy.

WHISKEY GINGER

WHISKEY GINGER

1½ oz. Buffalo Trace Bourbon
4 oz. Fentimans Ginger Beer
2 dashes of Peychaud's bitters
Pinch of grated fresh ginger
1 orange slice, for garnish

Fill a tumbler with ice and then add the bourbon, ginger beer, and bitters.

Top the cocktail with the ginger, garnish with the orange slice, and enjoy.

POMEGRANATE SMASH

2 oz. Maker's Mark 46 Bourbon
1 oz. pomegranate juice
½ oz. Honey Syrup (see page 64)
½ oz. fresh lemon juice
Pomegranate arils, for garnish

Place the bourbon, pomegranate juice, honey, and lemon juice in a cocktail shaker, fill it two-thirds of the way with ice, and shake until chilled.

Strain over ice into a rocks glass, garnish with the pomegranate arils, and enjoy.

PUNCH 415

1½ oz. Four Roses Bourbon
¾ oz. fresh lime juice
½ oz. Orgeat (see page 103)
2 oz. pineapple juice
5 dashes of Angostura bitters
Fresh mint, for garnish

Place the bourbon, lime juice, Orgeat, pineapple juice, and bitters in a cocktail shaker, fill it two-thirds of the way with ice, and shake until chilled.

Strain over ice into a rocks glass, garnish with fresh mint, and enjoy.

DERBY SEASON

2 oz. Kentucky bourbon
¾ oz. fresh lemon juice
¾ oz. Simple Syrup (see page 16)
½ oz. dry rosé
1 strip of lemon peel, for garnish

Place the bourbon, lemon juice, and syrup in a mixing glass, fill it two-thirds of the way with ice, and stir until chilled.

Strain over ice into a wineglass and top with the rosé.

Garnish with the strip of lemon peel and enjoy.

BLACKBERRY SMASH

2 blackberries, plus 1 for garnish

6 to 8 fresh mint leaves, plus more for garnish

¼ oz. Honey Syrup (see page 64)

½ oz. fresh lemon juice

2 oz. bourbon

Splash of club soda

Place the blackberries, fresh mint, and syrup in a cocktail shaker and muddle.

Add ice, the lemon juice, and bourbon, and shake until chilled.

Double strain over crushed ice into a rocks glass and top with the club soda.

Garnish with the additional blackberry and fresh mint and enjoy.

KENTUCKY MAID

2 English cucumber slices, plus 1 for garnish

2 oz. Kentucky bourbon

6 fresh mint leaves, plus more for garnish

¾ oz. fresh lime juice

¾ oz. Simple Syrup (see page 16)

Place the cucumber slices in a cocktail shaker and muddle.

Add ice, the bourbon, fresh mint, lime juice, and syrup and shake until chilled.

Double strain over ice into a rocks glass, garnish with the additional cucumber and fresh mint, and enjoy.

A LA LOUISIANE

1¾ oz. rye whiskey

¾ oz. sweet vermouth

¼ oz. Bénédictine

3 dashes of absinthe

3 dashes of Peychaud's bitters

1 Luxardo maraschino cherry, for garnish

Chill a coupe in the freezer.

Place all of the ingredients, except for the garnish, in a mixing glass, fill it two-thirds of the way with ice, and stir until chilled.

Strain into the chilled coupe, garnish with the maraschino cherry, and enjoy.

SILVER 75

¾ oz. bourbon

½ oz. fresh lemon juice

½ oz. Simple Syrup (see page 16)

4 oz. sparkling wine

1 strip of lemon peel, for garnish

Place the bourbon, lemon juice, and syrup in a mixing glass, fill it two-thirds of the way with ice, and stir until chilled.

Strain into a wineglass and top with the sparkling wine.

Express the strip of lemon peel over the drink, garnish the drink with it, and enjoy.

A LA LOUISIANE

AUTUMN LEAVES

1¼ oz. bourbon

¼ oz. Antica Formula Sweet Vermouth

½ oz. Ramazzotti

Dash of Angostura bitters

1 strip of lemon peel, for garnish

Place the bourbon, vermouth, Ramazzotti, and bitters in a mixing glass, fill it two-thirds of the way with ice, and stir until chilled.

Strain over ice into a double rocks glass, express the strip of lemon peel over the drink, garnish the cocktail with it, and enjoy.

HEARTS ON FIRE

2 oz. bourbon

¾ oz. Chambord

½ oz. Luxardo maraschino liqueur

2 dashes of Bittermens Hellfire Habanero Shrub

2 brandy-soaked cherries, for garnish

Place the bourbon, Chambord, Luxardo, and shrub in a mixing glass, fill it two-thirds of the way with ice, and stir until chilled.

Strain into a cocktail glass, garnish with the cherries, and enjoy.

SKYSCRAPER

1½ oz. bourbon

½ oz. sweet vermouth

Club soda, to top

Place the bourbon and vermouth in a mixing glass, fill it two-thirds of the way with ice, and stir until chilled.

Strain over ice into a rocks glass, top with club soda, and enjoy.

A COWBOY'S BREAKFAST

½ oz. Bacon-Infused Maple Syrup (see recipe)

1½ oz. bourbon

½ oz. tequila

1 egg white

3 dashes of cherry bitters

3 dashes of liquid smoke

2 strips of Candied Bacon (see recipe), for garnish

Place the maple syrup, bourbon, tequila, egg white, bitters, and liquid smoke in a cocktail shaker and dry shake for 10 to 15 seconds.

Add ice and shake until chilled.

Strain into a coupe, garnish with the Candied Bacon, and enjoy.

Bacon-Infused Maple Syrup: Combine ½ cup maple syrup and ½ cup crispy bacon pieces in a mason jar and steep for at least 1 hour. Strain before using or storing.

Candied Bacon: Preheat the oven to 400°F. Combine ¾ cup brown sugar and 1 tablespoon maple syrup in a bowl and dredge 8 to 10 slices of bacon in the mixture. Place the bacon on a baking sheet and place the sheet in the oven. Bake until the bacon is crispy, 15 to 20 minutes, flipping the bacon over halfway through. Remove the bacon from the oven and let it cool completely before using.

THE ROBIN'S NEST

1 oz. Suntory Toki Japanese Whisky

½ oz. Plantation O.F.T.D. rum

½ oz. Cinnamon Syrup (see recipe)

½ oz. fresh lemon juice

¾ oz. pineapple juice

1 oz. Passion Fruit Honey (see recipe)

1 oz. cranberry juice

1 candied pineapple wedge, for garnish

1 Luxardo maraschino cherry, for garnish

Place all of the ingredients, except for the cranberry juice and garnishes, in a cocktail shaker, fill it two-thirds of the way with ice, and shake vigorously until chilled.

Strain over crushed ice into a Hurricane glass and top with the cranberry juice.

Garnish the cocktail with the candied pineapple wedge and maraschino cherry and enjoy.

Cinnamon Syrup: Place 1 cup water and 2 cinnamon sticks in a saucepan and bring the mixture to a boil. Add 2 cups sugar and stir until it has dissolved. Remove the pan from heat, cover it, and let the mixture steep at room temperature for 12 hours. Strain the syrup through cheesecloth before using or storing.

Passion Fruit Honey: Place 1 cup honey in a saucepan and warm it over medium heat until it is runny. Pour the honey into a mason jar, stir in 1 cup passion fruit puree, and let the mixture cool before using or storing in the refrigerator.

BLACK MANHATTAN

BLACK MANHATTAN

1½ oz. bourbon

2 to 3 dashes of Fee Brothers Black Walnut Bitters

1 oz. sweet vermouth

3 maraschino cherries, for garnish

Place the bourbon, bitters, and vermouth in a mixing glass, fill it two-thirds of the way with ice, and stir until chilled.

Strain into a coupe, skewer the maraschino cherries on a toothpick, garnish the cocktail with them, and enjoy.

THE O.G.O.F.

2 oz. cask-strength bourbon

½ oz. Demerara Syrup (see page 65)

2 dashes of Angostura bitters

2 dashes of Bittermens Xocolatl Mole Bitters

1 torched orange twist, for garnish

Place the bourbon, syrup, and bitters in a mixing glass, fill it two-thirds of the way with ice, and stir until chilled.

Strain into a rocks glass, garnish with the torched orange twist, and enjoy.

HOT APPLE CIDER

3 orange peels
30 to 40 whole cloves
8 cups apple cider
4 cups bourbon
5 cinnamon sticks

Cut the orange peels into rectangles and press the cloves into them.

Place the apple cider, bourbon, and cinnamon sticks in a slow cooker and cook on low for 2 hours, making sure the mixture does not come to a boil.

Strain the spiked cider into glasses, garnish each glass with a piece of clove-studded orange peel, and enjoy.

SEAHORSE

1 (750 ml) bottle of bourbon
16 cups orange juice
2 cups lemon juice
¼ oz. blood orange bitters
1 cup Simple Syrup (see page 16)
Luxardo maraschino cherries, for garnish

Place the bourbon, orange juice, lemon juice, bitters, and syrup in a large punch bowl and refrigerate the mixture for at least 1 hour.

Ladle the punch over large ice cubes into rocks glasses, garnish with maraschino cherries, and enjoy.

FRISCO

2 oz. rye whiskey
1 oz. fresh lemon juice
Splash of Bénédictine

Place all of the ingredients in a cocktail shaker, fill it two-thirds of the way with ice, and shake until chilled.

Strain into a cocktail glass and enjoy.

THE SMOKING GUN

½ oz. Orgeat (see page 103)
3 dashes of Angostura bitters
½ oz. water
2 oz. Vanilla-Infused Bourbon (see recipe)
½ oz. Amaro Averna
1 orange peel
2 Luxardo maraschino cherries, for garnish

Place the Orgeat, bitters, water, bourbon, and amaro in a mixing glass and express the oils from the orange peel into the mixture.

Fill the mixing glass two-thirds of the way with ice and stir until chilled.

Strain into a decanter, use a smoking gun filled with cherrywood to infuse the mixture with smoke, and swirl the decanter.

Slowly pour the mixture over a large ice cube into a rocks glass, garnish with the Luxardo maraschino cherries, and enjoy.

Vanilla-Infused Bourbon: Split 2 vanilla beans down the middle, place them in a 750-ml bottle of bourbon, and steep for at least 3 days. Strain the mixture when you are ready to use it or leave the beans inside the bottle if you prefer a stronger vanilla flavor.

WATER FOR ELEPHANTS RYE SWIZZLE

1½ oz. rye whiskey

Juice of 1 lime

4 dashes of Angostura bitters

1 oz. Velvet Falernum

1 lime wedge, for garnish

Fill a Collins glass with crushed ice, add the rye, lime juice, bitters, and falernum, and use the swizzle method (see page 9) to combine and chill the drink.

Garnish with the lime wedge and enjoy.

RYE SOUR

2½ oz. rye whiskey

1 oz. fresh lemon juice

½ oz. Simple Syrup (see page 16)

1 maraschino cherry, for garnish

1 lemon slice, for garnish

Place the whiskey, lemon juice, and syrup in a cocktail shaker, fill it two-thirds of the way with ice, and shake until chilled.

Strain over ice into a rocks glass, garnish with the maraschino cherry and lemon slice, and enjoy.

PREAKNESS

2 oz. rye whiskey
½ oz. Bénédictine
½ oz. sweet vermouth
4 dashes of Angostura bitters

Place all of the ingredients in a cocktail shaker, fill it two-thirds of the way with ice, and shake until chilled.

Strain into a rocks glass and enjoy.

WAX & WANE

1 cedar wrap
2 oz. rye whiskey
½ oz. fresh lemon juice
½ oz. Demerara Syrup **(see page 65)**
4 dashes of Angostura bitters
1 egg white
6 fresh basil leaves
1 sprig of fresh rosemary, for garnish

Ignite the cedar wrap and quickly extinguish the flame.

Place the whiskey, lemon juice, syrup, bitters, egg white, and fresh basil in a cocktail shaker, fill it two-thirds of the way with ice, and shake until chilled.

Double strain into a Collins glass, garnish with the cedar wrap and fresh rosemary, and enjoy.

ANANDA SPRITZ

5 pineapple chunks

1½ oz. Knob Creek Bourbon

1 oz. Amaro Nonino

3 dashes of Angostura bitters

½ oz. Demerara Syrup (see page 65)

½ oz. fresh lemon juice

½ oz. pineapple juice

¾ oz. sparkling wine

Edible flower blossoms, for garnish

Place the pineapple in a cocktail shaker and muddle it.

Add all of the remaining ingredients, except for the sparkling wine and garnish, fill the shaker two-thirds of the way with ice, and shake until chilled.

Strain the cocktail into a cocktail glass and top with the sparkling wine.

Garnish with edible flower blossoms and enjoy.

FALCON SMASH

2 oz. rye whiskey

1 oz. fresh lemon juice

6 fresh basil leaves, plus more for garnish

1 oz. Simple Syrup (see page 16)

Place the whiskey, lemon juice, fresh basil, and syrup in a rocks glass and muddle.

Add ice and stir until chilled.

Garnish with additional fresh basil and enjoy.

ANANDA SPRITZ

WHISKEY DENNIS

2 oz. bourbon

½ oz. apricot liqueur

½ oz. apricot preserves

½ oz. Peychaud's Aperitivo

¼ oz. fresh lemon juice

¼ oz. fresh lime juice

2 dashes of Angostura bitters

Chill a coupe in the freezer.

Place all of the ingredients in a cocktail shaker, fill it two-thirds of the way with ice, and shake until chilled.

Double strain into the chilled coupe and enjoy.

PASSING DEADLINE

1½ oz. bourbon

½ oz. Cocchi Vermouth di Torino

½ oz. Lustau East India Solera Sherry

½ oz. Salers Gentiane Aperitif

1 bar spoon Demerara Syrup (see page 65)

Dash of Angostura bitters

Dash of Bittermens Xocolatl Mole Bitters

1 cinnamon stick, for garnish

Place the bourbon, vermouth, sherry, aperitif, syrup, and bitters in a mixing glass, fill it two-thirds of the way with ice, and stir until chilled.

Strain over ice into a rocks glass, garnish with the cinnamon stick, and enjoy.

JOHNNY'S BOILERMAKER SHOTS

4 cups Mellow Corn Whiskey
1¼ cups filtered water
1 cup Orange & Cherry Syrup (see recipe)
1 oz. Angostura bitters
Salt, for the rim
Sugar, for the rim
Orange slices, for garnish

Place the whiskey, water, syrup, and bitters in a large mason jar and stir to combine. Chill the mixture in the refrigerator for 2 hours.

To serve, rim shot glasses with salt and sugar and pour the cocktail into the glasses. Garnish each glass with an orange slice and enjoy.

Orange & Cherry Syrup: Combine 1 cup syrup from a jar of Luxardo maraschino cherries and 1 orange peel in a saucepan and bring to a gentle simmer. Remove the pan from heat and steep until the syrup has cooled completely. Strain before using or storing.

THIRD COAST MULE

1½ oz. Texas whiskey
¾ oz. fresh lemon juice
¾ oz. Simple Syrup (see page 16)
2 oz. ginger beer
2 oz. coconut water
1 strip of lemon peel, for garnish

Place the whiskey, lemon juice, and syrup in a cocktail shaker, fill it two-thirds of the way with ice, and shake until chilled.

Strain over ice into a Collins glass and top with the ginger beer and coconut water.

Express the strip of lemon peel over the drink, garnish the cocktail with it, and enjoy.

THROWING SHADE

1½ oz. Japanese whisky

¾ oz. fresh grapefruit juice

½ oz. Zucca Rabarbaro

½ oz. Ginger Syrup (see page 97)

Dash of Peychaud's bitters

Chill a coupe in the freezer.

Place all of the ingredients in a cocktail shaker, fill it two-thirds of the way with ice, and shake until chilled.

Double strain into the chilled coupe and enjoy.

HILL COUNTRY HIGHBALL

¾ oz. Rosemary Syrup (see recipe)

2 oz. Texas whiskey

Waterloo sparkling water, to top

1 sprig of fresh rosemary, for garnish

1 strip of grapefruit peel, for garnish

Fill a highball glass with ice, add the syrup and whiskey, and stir until chilled.

Top with sparkling water, garnish with the fresh rosemary and strip of grapefruit peel, and enjoy.

Rosemary Syrup: Place 1 cup sugar, 1 cup water, and 3 sprigs of fresh rosemary in a small saucepan and simmer the mixture for 10 to 15 minutes, stirring occasionally. Remove the pan from heat, strain, and let the syrup cool before using or storing.

GRAPES OF WRATH

1¾ oz. American whiskey

¾ oz. Simple Syrup (see page 16)

⅔ oz. fresh lemon juice

1 oz. egg white

¾ oz. Chateau Ste. Michelle Syrah

1 orange wheel, for garnish

1 maraschino cherry, for garnish

Place the whiskey, syrup, lemon juice, and egg white in a cocktail shaker and dry shake for 10 to 15 seconds.

Double strain over ice into a rocks glass and float the Syrah on top, pouring it slowly over the back of a spoon.

Garnish with the orange wheel and maraschino cherry and enjoy.

SOUTHERN SHIPWRECK

Sugar, for the rim

1 oz. Smith & Cross Traditional Jamaica Rum

1 oz. whiskey

¾ oz. fresh lime juice

¾ oz. Orgeat (see page 103)

¼ oz. Demerara Syrup (see page 65)

5 dashes of chocolate bitters

Wet the rim of a coupe and rim it with sugar.

Place the remaining ingredients in a cocktail shaker, fill it two-thirds of the way with ice, and shake until chilled.

Strain into the rimmed coupe and enjoy.

TARRAGUEUR

TARRAGUEUR

1½ oz. whiskey

1 oz. ruby red grapefruit juice

½ oz. Honey Syrup (see page 64)

1 small strip of grapefruit peel

8 fresh tarragon leaves, plus more for garnish

Dash of 10 Percent Saline Solution (see page 64)

Place the whiskey, grapefruit juice, syrup, strip of grapefruit peel, fresh tarragon, and saline solution in a cocktail shaker, add a large ice cube, and shake until chilled.

Strain into a Nick & Nora glass, garnish with additional fresh tarragon, and enjoy.

SHRUB YOU THE RIGHT WAY

¾ oz. Peach Shrub (see recipe)

2 oz. Maker's Mark Bourbon

½ oz. fresh lemon juice

½ oz. almond liqueur

Dash of peach bitters

Fresh mint, for garnish

Place the shrub, bourbon, lemon juice, liqueur, and bitters in a cocktail shaker, fill it two-thirds of the way with ice, and shake until chilled.

Strain into a rocks glass, garnish with the fresh mint, and enjoy.

Peach Shrub: Combine equal parts peach puree, sugar, and sherry vinegar in a saucepan and bring to a simmer, stirring to dissolve the sugar. Cook for 5 minutes, remove the pan from heat, and let the shrub cool before using or storing.

PEACHY KEANE

1 oz. bourbon

½ oz. Giffard Crème de Pêche de Vigne

½ oz. ginger liqueur

¾ oz. Honey Syrup (see page 64)

¾ oz. fresh lemon juice

1 egg white

1 dehydrated peach slice, for garnish

1 piece of candied ginger, for garnish

Place the bourbon, liqueurs, syrup, lemon juice, and egg white in a cocktail shaker and dry shake for 10 to 15 seconds.

Add ice and shake until chilled.

Double strain over ice into a rocks glass, garnish with the dehydrated peach slice and candied ginger, and enjoy.

KILL GIL

2 oz. Tennessee whiskey

¼ oz. Bénédictine

¾ oz. Tempus Fugit Spirits Gran Classico Bitter

1 strip of orange peel, for garnish

Place the whiskey, Bénédictine, and Tempus Fugit Gran Classico in a mixing glass, fill it two-thirds of the way with ice, and stir until chilled.

Strain over a large ice cube into a rocks glass and express the strip of orange peel over the drink.

Garnish the cocktail with the strip of orange peel and enjoy.

KAMEHAMEHA

1 oz. Suntory Toki Whisky

½ oz. shochu

½ oz. rye whiskey

½ oz. Punt e Mes

2 dashes of Angostura bitters

1 lemon twist, for garnish

Place a large ice cube in a rocks glass, add the whisky, shochu, rye, vermouth, and bitters, and stir until chilled.

Garnish with the lemon twist and enjoy.

OLD TIMER

1½ oz. bourbon

½ oz. Cynar

½ oz. Punt e Mes

½ oz. fresh lemon juice

¼ oz. Simple Syrup (see page 16)

2 to 4 dashes of Angostura bitters

Club soda, to top

1 orange twist, for garnish

Place the bourbon, Cynar, vermouth, lemon juice, syrup, and bitters in a cocktail shaker, fill it two-thirds of the way with ice, and shake until chilled.

Double strain over ice into a Collins glass and top with club soda.

Garnish with the orange twist and enjoy.

SAZERAC

Herbsaint, to rinse

1 sugar cube

3 dashes of Peychaud's bitters

1½ oz. rye whiskey

1 strip of lemon peel, for garnish

Rinse a rocks glass with Herbsaint and discard any excess. Chill the rocks glass in the freezer.

Place the sugar cube and bitters in a mixing glass and muddle.

Add the whiskey and stir until combined.

Strain into the chilled rocks glass, garnish with the strip of lemon peel, and enjoy.

WITHOUT A TRACE

Absinthe, to rinse

1½ oz. bourbon

½ oz. Amaro Nonino

½ oz. Honey Syrup (see page 64)

½ oz. fresh lemon juice

1 strip of orange peel, for garnish

Rinse a rocks glass with absinthe and discard any excess. Add a large ice cube to the glass.

Place the bourbon, amaro, syrup, and lemon juice in a mixing glass, fill it two-thirds of the way with ice, and stir until chilled.

Strain over ice into the rocks glass, garnish with the strip of orange peel, and enjoy.

SAZERAC

VANILLA SMASH

2 lemon wedges
6 to 8 fresh mint leaves
1 oz. Jim Beam Vanilla

Place the lemon wedges and mint leaves in a double rocks glass and muddle.

Add ice and the Jim Beam Vanilla, stir until chilled, and enjoy.

THE BAUDIN

1½ oz. bourbon
¾ oz. Honey Syrup (see page 64)
½ oz. fresh lemon juice
Dash of Tabasco
1 strip of lemon peel, for garnish

Place the bourbon, syrup, lemon juice, and hot sauce in a cocktail shaker, fill it two-thirds of the way with ice, and shake until chilled.

Strain over ice into a rocks glass, garnish with the strip of lemon peel, and enjoy.

THE PEACEFUL PEOPLE

1½ oz. Balcones Baby Blue Corn Whisky

1 teaspoon mezcal

¾ oz. Toasted Butter Pecan Syrup (see recipe)

½ oz. fresh lemon juice

3 dashes of coffee bitters

Place all of the ingredients in a cocktail shaker, fill it two-thirds of the way with ice, and shake until chilled.

Strain into a rocks glass and enjoy.

Toasted Butter Pecan Syrup: Preheat the oven to 350°F. Place ½ cup pecans on a baking sheet and toast them in the oven for 5 minutes. Remove from the oven, let them cool slightly, and then pulse in a food processor. Combine the pecans and 1¼ cups water and let the mixture steep for 2 hours. Place the mixture in a food processor or blender, puree until smooth, and strain through cheesecloth while gently squeezing to remove as much liquid as possible. Add the 1 cup caster (superfine) sugar and stir until it has dissolved. Add 2 teaspoons melted butter, stir to combine, and use as desired.

RUM

As it is easily the most diverse spirit on Earth, the prospect of working with rum while making cocktails is a fun one. But it also can be overwhelming, with offerings from more than 60 countries available to sample.

If you're ever wondering what to select from the dizzying array available, here's a helpful précis: blended rums that have been lightly aged (1 to 4 years) are good go-to's for mixing, and rums in this age range have been rested long enough to let the nature of the spirit come through, but not long enough to take on too much influence from the barrel. That said, there are more than a few instances where a more mature rum, aged from 5 to 14 years, is called for. For those familiar with the higher price tags that extended aging can come with, rest assured—these aged rums, which are also wonderful for sipping neat, carry a much lower price tag than similarly aged Scotches or bourbons. These older options are especially worth considering in tiki cocktails, where you want as much complexity as possible.

LEMONGRASS MOJITO

2 teaspoons loose-leaf lemongrass tea

6 fresh mint leaves

1¾ oz. rum

¾ oz. Simple Syrup (see page 16)

¾ oz. apple juice

¾ oz. fresh lime juice

1⅜ oz. seltzer water

1 lemongrass stalk, for garnish

Place the loose-leaf tea in 1½ oz. hot water and steep for 4 minutes.

Add the mint leaves to a Collins glass and muddle. Strain the tea into the glass, add the rum, syrup, apple juice, and lime juice, and stir until the mixture is at room temperature.

Add ice and top with the seltzer.

Garnish with the lemongrass stalk and enjoy.

MARY PICKFORD

2 oz. rum

1½ oz. pineapple juice

1 bar spoon grenadine

1 bar spoon Luxardo maraschino liqueur

2 Luxardo maraschino cherries, for garnish

Chill a coupe in the freezer.

Place all of the ingredients, except for the garnish, in a cocktail shaker, fill it two-thirds of the way with ice, and shake until chilled.

Strain the cocktail into the chilled coupe, skewer the maraschino cherries on a toothpick, garnish the cocktail with them, and enjoy.

THE FRUIT STAND

1½ oz. Plantation Stiggins' Fancy Pineapple Rum

½ oz. Giffard Abricot du Roussillon

1 oz. pineapple juice

½ oz. fresh lime juice

¼ oz. Simple Syrup (see page 16)

4 dashes of Peychaud's bitters

Place all of the ingredients, except for the bitters, in a cocktail shaker, fill it two-thirds of the way with ice, and shake until chilled.

Double strain into two shot glasses, top each shot with the bitters, and enjoy.

POLAR SHORT CUT

1⅓ oz. aged rum

2 bar spoons Cointreau

2 bar spoons cherry brandy

⅔ oz. dry vermouth

Place all of the ingredients in a mixing glass, fill it two-thirds of the way with ice, and stir until chilled.

Strain into a cocktail glass and enjoy.

DOT LINE

¼ oz. ground Kenyan coffee
1⅓ oz. Bacardí Carta Blanca rum
⅔ oz. umeshu
1 bar spoon Pedro Ximénez sherry
1 bar spoon St-Germain
Dash of balsamic vinegar

Place a coffee dripper over a mixing glass, line the coffee dripper with a filter, and place the coffee in the filter.

Pour the rum, umeshu, sherry, and St-Germain over the coffee and let them drip into the glass.

Add the balsamic vinegar to the mixing glass, then ice, and stir to incorporate.

Strain over an ice sphere into a rocks glass and enjoy.

ZACAPA MARTINI

2 oz. Ron Zacapa No. 23 rum
1 bar spoon Bulleit Bourbon
2 Griottines, for garnish

Place the rum and bourbon in a mixing glass, fill it two-thirds of the way with ice, and stir until chilled.

Strain into a rocks glass, garnish with the Griottines, and enjoy.

SECRET LIFE OF PLANTS

SECRET LIFE OF PLANTS

1½ oz. lightly aged rum

¾ oz. Mango & Oolong Syrup (see recipe)

¾ oz. fresh lime juice

¼ oz. Orgeat (see page 103)

¼ oz. Falernum

10 drops of 10 Percent Saline Solution (see page 64)

Dash of absinthe

Fresh Thai basil, for garnish

Place all of the ingredients, except for the garnish, in a cocktail shaker, fill it two-thirds of the way with ice, and shake until chilled.

Fill a tumbler with crushed ice and strain the cocktail over it.

Top with more crushed ice, garnish with fresh Thai basil, and enjoy.

Mango & Oolong Syrup: Place ¾ cup water in a saucepan and heat it to 195°F. Add ¼ cup loose-leaf oolong tea and steep for 5 minutes. Strain the tea, discard the leaves, and return the tea to the saucepan. Add 30 oz. mango puree, 30 oz. sugar, 1 (12 oz.) can of mango nectar, and a scant 2½ teaspoons citric acid and warm the mixture over low heat, stirring to dissolve the sugar. When the syrup is well combined, remove the pan from heat and let it cool completely before using or storing.

JUNGLE BIRD

2 oz. Smith & Cross Traditional Jamaica Rum

¾ oz. Campari

1½ oz. pineapple juice

½ oz. fresh lime juice

1 pineapple wedge, for garnish

Place all of the ingredients, except for the garnish, in a cocktail shaker, fill it two-thirds of the way with ice, and shake until chilled.

Fill a rocks glass with ice and strain the cocktail over it.

Garnish the cocktail with the pineapple wedge and enjoy.

PAINKILLER

2½ oz. overproof rum
1 oz. cream of coconut
1 oz. orange juice
4 oz. pineapple juice
1 orange slice, for garnish
1 cinnamon stick, for garnish
Freshly grated nutmeg, for garnish

Place all of the ingredients, except for the garnishes, in a cocktail shaker, fill it halfway with crushed ice, and shake vigorously until chilled.

Pour the contents of the shaker into a tiki mug, garnish with the orange slice, cinnamon stick, and freshly grated nutmeg, and enjoy.

FOG CUTTER

1½ oz. fresh lemon juice
1½ oz. fresh orange juice
½ oz. Orgeat (see page 103)
1 oz. pisco
½ oz. London dry gin
2 oz. aged rum
½ oz. oloroso sherry
Fresh mint, for garnish

Place all of the ingredients, except for the sherry and garnish, in a cocktail shaker, fill it two-thirds of the way with ice, and shake vigorously until chilled.

Fill a tiki mug with crushed ice and strain the cocktail over it.

Float the sherry on top of the cocktail, pouring it slowly over the back of a spoon.

Garnish with fresh mint and enjoy.

ZOMBIE

1½ oz. Appleton Estate Signature Jamaica Rum

1½ oz. Smith & Cross Traditional Jamaica Rum

1 oz. 151-proof rum

6 drops of absinthe

½ oz. Falernum

1 bar spoon grenadine

½ oz. Don's Mix (see recipe)

¾ oz. fresh lime juice

Dash of Angostura bitters

Fresh mint, for garnish

1 spent lime shell, for garnish

Place all of the ingredients, except for the garnishes, in a cocktail shaker, fill it two-thirds of the way with ice, and shake vigorously until chilled.

Fill a tiki mug with crushed ice and strain the cocktail over it.

Garnish with fresh mint and the lime shell and enjoy.

Don's Mix: Place ½ cup Cinnamon Syrup (see page 262), ½ cup Honey Syrup (see page 64), and 1 cup grapefruit juice in a large mason jar and stir to combine. Use as desired.

THREE DOTS AND A DASH

1½ oz. rhum agricole

½ oz. lightly aged rum

¼ oz. St. Elizabeth Allspice Dram

½ oz. Velvet Falernum

½ oz. Honey Syrup (see page 64)

½ oz. fresh orange juice

½ oz. fresh lime juice

3 Luxardo maraschino cherries, for garnish

2 pineapple leaves, for garnish

Place all of the ingredients, except for the garnishes, in a cocktail shaker, fill it two-thirds of the way with ice, and shake vigorously until chilled.

Strain over ice into a Collins glass.

Thread the maraschino cherries onto a skewer, garnish the cocktail with the cherries and pineapple leaves, and enjoy.

DAUPHIN

1½ oz. Goslings Black Seal Rum

2 dashes of Miracle Mile Bitters Co. Chocolate Chili Bitters

½ oz. Demerara Syrup (see page 65)

½ oz. Ancho Reyes

1 oz. absinthe

1¼ oz. toasted coconut almond milk

Cacao nibs, for garnish

1 star anise pod, for garnish

Place a Collins glass in a bowl and build the cocktail in the glass, adding the ingredients, except for the garnishes, in the order they are listed.

Fill the bowl and the glass with pebble ice and stir the cocktail until it is chilled and combined.

Garnish with cacao nibs and the star anise and enjoy.

DAUPHIN

PLANTER'S PUNCH

2 oz. rum
½ oz. grenadine
¼ oz. Demerara Syrup (see page 65)
¼ oz. St. Elizabeth Allspice Dram
½ oz. fresh lime juice
2 dashes of Angostura bitters
1 edible orchid blossom, for garnish

Place all of the ingredients, except for the bitters and garnish, in a cocktail shaker, fill it two-thirds of the way with ice, and shake vigorously until chilled.

Strain over ice into a Collins glass and top with the bitters.

Garnish with the edible orchid and enjoy.

DOCTOR FUNK

½ oz. fresh lemon juice
¼ oz. grenadine
½ oz. fresh lime juice
½ oz. Demerara Syrup (see page 65)
Dash of Pernod
Dash of Angostura bitters
2¼ oz. black rum
1 oz. seltzer
2 pineapple leaves, for garnish

Place all of the ingredients, except for the garnish, in a cocktail shaker, fill it two-thirds of the way with ice, and shake vigorously until chilled.

Fill a Collins glass with crushed ice and strain the cocktail over it.

Garnish with the pineapple leaves and enjoy.

HURRICANE

1 oz. black rum

1 oz. Jamaican rum

1¼ oz. Passion Fruit Blend (see recipe)

¼ oz. fresh lemon juice

Dash of Peychaud's bitters

1 lemon wheel, for garnish

Place all of the ingredients, except for the garnish, in a cocktail shaker, fill it two-thirds of the way with crushed ice, and shake vigorously for three times as long as usual.

Pour the contents of the shaker into a Hurricane glass, garnish with the lemon wheel, and enjoy.

Passion Fruit Blend: Place 15 oz. passion fruit puree, 1 lb. caster (superfine) sugar, and 6⅓ oz. Campari in a large mason jar and stir until the sugar has dissolved. Use as desired.

CARIBBEAN MILK PUNCH

1 oz. Vanilla Syrup (see page 52)

1 oz. rum

½ oz. bourbon

1 oz. heavy cream

Freshly grated nutmeg, for garnish

Place all of the ingredients, except for the garnish, in a cocktail shaker, fill it two-thirds of the way with ice, and shake vigorously until chilled.

Strain over ice into a tumbler, garnish with the nutmeg, and enjoy.

MAI TAI

There is some debate over where and when the Mai Tai was created, with various factions arguing for each of the tiki dons—Don the Beachcomber and Trader Vic—as the progenitor. This version favors the latter, but only because the origin story is better. According to legend, Vic whipped it up and served it to two friends visiting from Tahiti. One of them, Carrie Guild, according to Trader Vic's lore, took a sip and replied, "Mai tai—roa ae." Translated from Tahitian, that means, "Out of this world—the best."

2 oz. aged rum
¾ oz. curaçao
½ oz. Orgeat (see page 103)
½ oz. fresh lime juice
¼ oz. Rock Candy Syrup (see recipe)
Fresh mint, for garnish
1 spent lime shell, for garnish

Place all of the ingredients, except for the garnishes, in a cocktail shaker, fill it two-thirds of the way with crushed ice, and shake vigorously until chilled.

Pour the contents of the shaker into a Mai Tai glass, garnish with the mint and spent lime shell, and enjoy.

Rock Candy Syrup: Place ½ cup water in a small saucepan and bring it to a boil. Add 1 cup turbinado sugar and stir until it has dissolved. Add 1 cinnamon stick and 2 whole cloves and return the syrup to a boil. Reduce the heat and simmer the syrup for 15 minutes. Remove the pan from heat and let the syrup cool completely. Strain before using or storing in the refrigerator, where the syrup will keep for up to 6 months.

TRADER VI

MISSIONARY'S DOWNFALL

1 oz. aged rum

½ oz. apricot liqueur

½ oz. Honey & Cinnamon Syrup (see recipe)

½ oz. grapefruit juice

1½ oz. pineapple juice

½ oz. fresh lime juice

10 to 15 fresh mint leaves, plus more for garnish

1 orange wheel, for garnish

Place all of the ingredients, except for the garnishes, in a cocktail shaker, add crushed ice, and flash mix with a hand blender.

Pour the contents of the shaker into a Hurricane glass, garnish with the orange wheel and additional mint, and enjoy.

Honey & Cinnamon Syrup: Place 1 cup water and 2 cinnamon sticks in a saucepan and bring the mixture to a boil. Add 1 cup honey and stir until it has liquefied. Remove the pan from heat. Cover the pan and let the syrup sit at room temperature for 12 hours. Strain the syrup through cheesecloth before using or storing in the refrigerator, where it will keep for up to 1 month.

DARK & STORMY

2 oz. black rum

4 oz. ginger beer

1 lime wedge, for garnish

Fill a rocks glass with ice, add the rum and ginger beer, and stir until chilled.

Garnish with the lime wedge and enjoy.

HURRICANE DROPS

1 oz. Plantation 3 Stars Rum

½ oz. gin

¾ oz. fresh lemon juice

1 oz. pineapple juice

1 oz. guava puree

¾ oz. Ginger Syrup (see page 97)

1 bar spoon Herbsaint

4 dashes of Angostura bitters

3 pineapple leaves, for garnish

1 edible orchid blossom, for garnish

Place all of the ingredients, except for the bitters and garnishes, in a mixing glass, add 2 oz. crushed ice, and stir until foamy.

Pour the contents of the mixing glass into a Collins glass, add the bitters, and top with more crushed ice.

Garnish with the pineapple leaves and orchid blossom and enjoy.

NAVY GROG

1 oz. Appleton Estate Signature Jamaica Rum

1 oz. Smith & Cross Traditional Jamaica Rum

1 oz. El Dorado 5-Year Rum

1 oz. Demerara Syrup (see page 65)

¾ oz. fresh lime juice

¾ oz. fresh grapefruit juice

¼ oz. St. Elizabeth Allspice Dram

1 spent lime shell, for garnish

Place all of the ingredients, except for the garnish, in a cocktail shaker, fill it two-thirds of the way with ice, and shake vigorously until chilled.

Fill a tumbler with crushed ice and strain the cocktail over it.

Garnish with the spent lime shell and enjoy.

JET PILOT

1 oz. Smith & Cross Traditional Jamaica Rum
¾ oz. Don Q Añejo Rum
6 dashes of Pernod
¾ oz. 151-proof rum
½ oz. Velvet Falernum
½ oz. Cinnamon Syrup (see page 262)
½ oz. white grapefruit juice
½ oz. fresh lime juice
Dash of Angostura bitters
1 Luxardo maraschino cherry, for garnish
2 pineapple leaves, for garnish
Fresh mint, for garnish

Place all of the ingredients, except for the garnishes, in a cocktail shaker, fill it two-thirds of the way with ice, and shake vigorously until chilled.

Fill a tumbler with pebble ice and strain the cocktail over it.

Garnish the cocktail with the maraschino cherry, pineapple leaves, and fresh mint and enjoy.

RUNAWAY RUM RUNNER PUNCH

1 oz. spiced rum
2 oz. orange juice
1 oz. cranberry-raspberry juice

Fill a highball glass with ice, add the rum and orange juice, and stir until chilled.

Top with the cranberry-raspberry juice, let it filter through the cocktail, and enjoy.

BAHAMA MAMA

½ oz. dark rum

¼ oz. 151-proof rum

½ oz. coconut liqueur

¼ oz. Kahlúa

Juice of ½ lemon

4 oz. pineapple juice

1 strawberry, for garnish

Place the rums, liqueur, Kahlúa, lemon juice, and pineapple juice in a cocktail shaker, fill it two-thirds of the way with ice, and shake until chilled.

Strain over ice into a highball glass, garnish with the strawberry, and enjoy.

IMPROVED PIÑA COLADA

2 oz. spiced rum

1½ oz. pineapple juice

2 oz. cream of coconut

½ oz. passion fruit puree

1 cup ice

½ oz. Campari

1 orange slice, for garnish

Place the rum, pineapple juice, cream of coconut, passion fruit puree, and ice in a blender and puree until smooth.

Pour into a Hurricane glass and float the Campari on top of the drink, pouring it slowly over the back of a spoon.

Garnish with the orange slice and enjoy.

GAMORA'S ZOMBIE

1 oz. Real McCoy 5-Year Rum

1 oz. Appleton Estate Signature Jamaica Rum

¼ oz. Marlo's Mix (see recipe)

¾ oz. Passion Fruit Syrup (see page 87)

¾ oz. ruby red grapefruit juice

¾ oz. fresh lime juice

¼ oz. absinthe

1 oz. Hamilton Guyana 151 Rum

Fresh mint, for garnish

1 Luxardo maraschino cherry, for garnish

1 lime wheel, for garnish

Place all of the ingredients, except for the 151-proof rum and garnishes, in a blender and puree until combined.

Fill a Zombie mug with pebble ice and pour the cocktail over it.

Float the 151-proof rum on top of the cocktail, pouring it slowly over the back of a spoon.

Garnish with the fresh mint, maraschino cherry, and lime wheel and enjoy.

Marlo's Mix: Place 1 cup St. Elizabeth Allspice Dram and 1 cup Cinnamon Syrup (see page 262) in a mason jar, cover it, and shake until combined. Use as desired.

THE PADDINGTON

Absinthe, to rinse
1½ oz. white rum
½ oz. fresh lemon juice
½ oz. grapefruit juice
½ oz. Lillet
1 bar spoon orange marmalade
1 grapefruit twist, for garnish

Rinse a coupe with absinthe and discard the excess.

Place the rum, juices, Lillet, and marmalade in a cocktail shaker, fill it two-thirds of the way with ice, and shake until chilled.

Strain into the rinsed coupe, garnish with the grapefruit twist, and enjoy.

SUN BREAKING THROUGH

¾ oz. Ten to One Caribbean Dark Rum
¾ oz. Fonseca 10-Year Tawny Port
¾ oz. Amaro Montenegro
¾ oz. fresh lime juice
¾ oz. Pineapple Syrup (see recipe)
1 edible flower blossom, for garnish

Place all of the ingredients, except for the garnish, in a cocktail shaker, fill it two-thirds of the way with ice, and shake until chilled.

Fill a Collins glass with crushed ice and strain the cocktail over it.

Garnish with the flower blossom and enjoy.

Pineapple Syrup: Combine equal parts pineapple juice and caster (superfine) sugar in a blender and puree on high for 2 minutes. Let the syrup settle, then transfer it to a container and chill in the refrigerator until ready to use.

THE EXPEDITION

2 oz. black blended rum (such as Coruba, Goslings, or Hamilton 86)
1 oz. bourbon
¼ oz. Bittermens New Orleans Coffee Liqueur
1 oz. fresh lime juice
½ oz. Cinnamon Syrup (see page 262)
½ oz. Honey Syrup (see page 64)
¼ oz. Vanilla Syrup (see page 52)
2 oz. seltzer
1 edible orchid blossom, for garnish

Place all of the ingredients, except for the garnish, in a cocktail shaker, add crushed ice and 4 to 6 small cubes, and flash mix with a hand blender.

Pour the contents of the shaker into a tiki mug.

Garnish with the edible orchid blossom and enjoy.

RUM BA BA

1½ oz. Jamaican rum
1½ oz. heavy cream
1 oz. Orgeat (see page 103)
½ oz. fresh lemon juice
1¼ oz. passion fruit puree
2 dashes of Peychaud's bitters
1 passion fruit slice, for garnish
Fresh mint, for garnish

Place all of the ingredients, except for the garnishes, in a cocktail shaker, fill it two-thirds of the way with ice, and shake until chilled.

Fill a rocks glass with ice and double strain the cocktail over it.

Garnish with the passion fruit slice and fresh mint and enjoy.

SECRET OF THE LOST LAGOON

1½ oz. Coruba Dark Rum
½ oz. Wray & Nephew Overproof Rum
¾ oz. fresh lime juice
½ oz. pineapple juice
½ oz. cold-brew coffee
½ oz. Ginger Syrup (see page 97)
¾ oz. Vanilla Syrup (see page 52)
1 pineapple leaf, for garnish
1 edible orchid blossom, for garnish

Place all of the ingredients, except for the garnishes, in a cocktail shaker, fill it halfway with crushed ice, and shake until chilled.

Pour the contents of the shaker into a double rocks glass, garnish with the pineapple leaf and edible orchid, and enjoy.

KILL DEVIL PUNCH

4 sugar cubes
1 oz. club soda
4 raspberries
1 oz. fresh lemon juice
2 oz. pineapple juice
2 oz. Jamaican rum
1½ oz. Champagne
1 lime wheel, for garnish

Place the sugar cubes, club soda, and raspberries in a mixing glass and muddle.

Add the juices, rum, and ice and stir until chilled.

Strain into a coupe and top with the Champagne.

Garnish with the lime wheel and enjoy.

THE POWER OF ONE

2 oz. Jamaican rum

1 oz. coconut milk

1 oz. fresh lime juice

1 oz. Demerara Syrup (see page 65)

1 teaspoon shaved fresh ginger, for garnish

Place all of the ingredients, except for the garnish, in a cocktail shaker, fill it two-thirds of the way with ice, and shake until chilled.

Fill a Collins glass with crushed ice and strain the cocktail over it.

Top with more crushed ice, garnish with the ginger, and enjoy.

PEDRO MARTINEZ COCKTAIL

1 small strip of lime peel

2 oz. demerara rum

1 oz. Cocchi Vermouth di Torino

¼ oz. maraschino liqueur

10 drops of Angostura bitters

3 dashes of orange bitters

4 drops of absinthe

2 strips of lemon peel

Express the strip of lime peel over a mixing glass and then drop the peel into the glass.

Add ice and all of the remaining ingredients, except for the strips of lemon peel, and stir until chilled.

Strain over a large ice cube into the rocks glass, express the strips of lemon peel over the drink, discard them, and enjoy.

MAI KINDA GAI

¾ oz. Banana & Cashew Orgeat (see recipe)
1½ oz. Hamilton 86 Demerara Rum
½ oz. Mandarine Napoléon Liqueur
1 oz. fresh lime juice
½ oz. Ron Zacapa No. 23 rum, to float
2 sprigs of fresh mint, for garnish
1 orange slice, for garnish
1 maraschino cherry, for garnish

Place the orgeat, Hamilton rum, liqueur, and lime juice in a cocktail shaker, fill it two-thirds of the way with ice, and shake until chilled.

Strain over ice into a rocks glass and float the Ron Zacapa on top, pouring it slowly over the back of a spoon.

Garnish with the fresh mint, orange slice, and maraschino cherry and enjoy.

Banana & Cashew Orgeat: In a saucepan, bring 1 cup cashew milk to a simmer. Place 2 cups sugar in a mason jar, pour the warmed cashew milk over it, and stir until the sugar has dissolved. Let cool and then stir in 4 oz. Giffard Banane du Brésil liqueur. Use as desired.

CUBA LIBRE

½ oz. fresh lime juice
1 lime twist
2 oz. unaged rum
Cola, to top

Fill a highball glass with ice, add the lime juice, lime twist, and rum, and stir until chilled.

Top with cola and enjoy.

TOM & JERRY

Dash of egg white

1 oz. Simple Syrup (see page 16)

1 oz. aged rum

1 oz. brandy

2 oz. warm milk

1 cinnamon stick, for garnish

Place the egg white, syrup, rum, brandy, and warm milk in a mug and stir to combine.

Garnish with the cinnamon stick and enjoy.

THE PINK FLAMINGO

Splash of Fernet-Branca Reduction (see recipe)

1½ oz. Banks 5 Island Rum

½ oz. Liber & Co. Pineapple Gum Syrup

1 oz. hibiscus tea

½ oz. condensed milk

½ oz. cream of coconut

½ cup ice

Place the Fernet-Branca Reduction in a Daiquiri glass.

Place the rum, gum syrup, tea, milk, cream of coconut, and ice in a blender and puree until smooth.

Pour the cocktail into the Daiquiri glass and enjoy.

Fernet-Branca Reduction: In a saucepan, combine equal parts Fernet-Branca and sugar and cook over medium heat until the mixture has been reduced to a syrup. Let the reduction cool completely before using or storing in the refrigerator.

MOJITO

1 tablespoon caster (superfine) sugar

Juice of ½ lime

1 cup crushed ice

10 fresh mint leaves

2 oz. unaged rum

6 oz. club soda

3 to 6 sprigs of fresh mint, for garnish

2 lime wheels, for garnish

Place the sugar and lime juice in a Collins glass and muddle until the sugar has dissolved.

Add one-quarter of the crushed ice and rub the fresh mint leaves over the rim of the glass.

Tear the mint leaves in half, add them to the glass, and stir until combined.

Add the remaining ice, the rum, and the club soda and stir until chilled.

Garnish with the sprigs of fresh mint and lime wheels and enjoy.

COCONUT RUM PUNCH

1 oz. unaged rum

1 oz. coconut rum

Juice of ½ lime

Dash of Angostura bitters

2 oz. orange juice

2 oz. pineapple juice

2 pineapple chunks, for garnish

Fill a highball glass with ice, add the rums, lime juice, bitters, orange juice, and pineapple juice, and stir until chilled.

Garnish with the pineapple chunks and enjoy.

PRIVATEER

½ lime, cut into wedges

1 oz. coconut rum

3 oz. cola

1 lime wheel, for garnish

Squeeze the juice from the lime wedges into a highball glass and then add the spent lime wedges to the glass.

Add the rum, cola, and ice and stir until chilled.

Garnish with the lime wheel and enjoy.

COOL SUMMER

5 fresh mint leaves, torn

Juice of 1 lime wedge

1 oz. unaged rum

2 oz. lemonade

1 lemon wheel, for garnish

Place the fresh mint and lime juice in a highball glass and muddle.

Add the rum, lemonade, and ice and stir until chilled.

Top with more ice, garnish with the lemon wheel, and enjoy.

CAPRI C'EST FINI

4 cherry tomatoes, plus 1 for garnish

2 fresh basil leaves, plus 1 for garnish

½ oz. fresh lemon juice

½ oz. Simple Syrup (see page 16)

½ teaspoon balsamic vinegar

½ oz. aged rum

1 mozzarella ball, for garnish

Chill a coupe in the freezer.

Place the tomatoes and basil leaves in a cocktail shaker and muddle.

Add ice, the lemon juice, syrup, vinegar, and rum and shake until chilled.

Double strain into the chilled coupe, garnish with the mozzarella ball and additional tomato and fresh basil, and enjoy.

HAITIAN DIVORCE

1½ oz. Haitian rum

¾ oz. mezcal

½ oz. Pedro Ximénez sherry

2 dashes of Angostura bitters

1 orange twist, for garnish

1 lime twist, for garnish

Fill a rocks glass with large ice cubes, add the rum, mezcal, sherry, and bitters, and stir until chilled.

Garnish with the orange twist and lime twist and enjoy.

BEHIND GOD'S BACK

¼ oz. Simple Syrup (see page 16)
¼ oz. Cinnamon Syrup (see page 262)
¼ oz. Orgeat (see page 103)
½ oz. pineapple juice
¾ oz. fresh lime juice
2 oz. aged rum
2 dashes of Peychaud's bitters
2 dashes of Angostura bitters
Fresh mint, for garnish

Fill a Hurricane glass with crushed ice, add the syrups, Orgeat, juices, and rum, and use the swizzle method (see page 9) to combine.

Add more crushed ice and top with the bitters.

Garnish with fresh mint and enjoy.

OLD CUBAN

6 fresh mint leaves
½ oz. fresh lime juice
1⅓ oz. Havana Club rum
½ oz. Simple Syrup (see page 16)
1 teaspoon Ginger Syrup (see page 97)
Champagne, to top
2 dashes of Angostura bitters

Chill a cocktail glass in the freezer.

Place the fresh mint, lime juice, rum, and syrups in a cocktail shaker, fill it two-thirds of the way with ice, and shake until chilled.

Strain into the chilled cocktail glass, top with Champagne and the bitters, and enjoy.

FALLEN ANGEL

3 sprigs of fresh mint, plus more for garnish

½ oz. fresh lime juice

1 oz. pineapple juice

½ oz. Honey Syrup (see page 64)

½ oz. banana liqueur

1½ oz. Ron Zacapa No. 23 rum

Banana Dolphin (see recipe), for garnish

Place the mint in a cocktail shaker and gently muddle. Add all of the remaining ingredients, except for the garnish, and three ice cubes to the shaker and whip shake until chilled.

Fill a wineglass with crushed ice and strain the cocktail over it.

Garnish the cocktail with the Banana Dolphin and additional mint and enjoy.

Banana Dolphin: Cut the bottom fifth off of a banana. Slice off ¼ inch of the stem tip of the banana, and slice through the stem to make the dolphin's mouth. Make a slit on the bottom of the banana, about 1 inch in from where you made your initial cut. You want to make sure this slit goes to the equator of the banana, as this will help the garnish stay on the rim of the glass. Insert one clove on each side of the banana, above the dolphin's mouth, affix the garnish to the glass, and enjoy.

ROSES ARE FREE

1 oz. unaged rum

1 oz. triple sec

2 oz. club soda

Splash of grenadine

1 maraschino cherry, for garnish

Fill a rocks glass with ice, add the rum and triple sec, and stir until chilled.

Top with the club soda and grenadine, garnish with the maraschino cherry, and enjoy.

LAWYERS, GUNS & MONEY

2 dashes of Amargo Chuncho Bitters

2 dashes of Bittermens Hellfire Habanero Shrub

¼ oz. crème de cacao

½ oz. port

½ oz. Pedro Ximénez sherry

½ oz. Haitian rum

1½ oz. red wine

1 orange twist, for garnish

Spicy Chocolate Mixture (see recipe), for garnish

Place the bitters, shrub, crème de cacao, port, sherry, rum, and red wine in a cocktail shaker, fill it two-thirds of the way with ice, and shake until chilled.

Strain over ice into a rocks glass, garnish with the orange twist and Spicy Chocolate Mixture, and enjoy.

Spicy Chocolate Mixture: Combine equal parts cocoa powder, chili powder, and sugar in a small dish and use as desired.

OCHO OLD FASHIONED

3 dashes of Tobacco-Infused Bitters (see recipe)
2 oz. Bacardí Ocho rum
½ oz. Demerara Syrup (see page 65)
1 dried tobacco leaf, for garnish

Place the bitters, rum, and syrup in a mixing glass, fill it two-thirds of the way with ice, and gently stir until chilled.

Strain over ice into a rocks glass, garnish with the dried tobacco leaf, and enjoy.

Tobacco-Infused Bitters: Steep 1 or 2 tobacco leaves in a 6.7 oz. bottle of Angostura bitters for 3 to 5 hours. Strain before using or storing.

THE ESCAPE

2 oz. aged rum
1 oz. pineapple juice
1 oz. cream of coconut
¾ oz. sweet vermouth
1 pineapple chunk, for garnish
1 maraschino cherry, for garnish

Place the rum, juice, and cream of coconut in a cocktail shaker, fill it two-thirds of the way with ice, and shake until chilled.

Strain over crushed ice into a goblet and float the vermouth on top, pouring it slowly over the back of a spoon.

Garnish with the pineapple chunk and maraschino cherry and enjoy.

HEMINGWAY DAIQUIRI

1½ oz. lightly aged rum

¼ oz. Luxardo maraschino liqueur

¾ oz. fresh lime juice

¼ oz. grapefruit juice

1 lime wheel, for garnish

Chill a coupe in the freezer.

Place the rum, liqueur, and juices in a cocktail shaker, fill it two-thirds of the way with ice, and shake until chilled.

Strain into the chilled coupe, garnish with the lime wheel, and enjoy.

ROMEO À RIO

½ oz. Red Fruit Syrup (see recipe)

½ oz. fresh lemon juice

1¾ oz. cachaça

1 teaspoon crème de violette

2 sprigs of fresh mint

1 egg white

Dash of smoked paprika, for garnish

Chill a cocktail glass in the freezer.

Place the syrup, juice, cachaça, crème de violette, fresh mint, and egg white in a cocktail shaker and dry shake for 15 seconds.

Add ice and shake until chilled.

Strain into the chilled cocktail glass, garnish with the smoked paprika, and enjoy.

Red Fruit Syrup: Add ½ cup raspberries and ½ cup strawberries to a Simple Syrup (see page 16) once it has come to a simmer. Cook for 5 minutes, pressing down on the berries with a wooden spoon. Remove the pan from heat and let the syrup cool completely. Strain before using or storing.

NACIONAL

¾ oz. Nacional Biz (see recipe)
¾ oz. fresh lime juice
½ oz. pineapple juice
½ oz. Yuzu Syrup (see recipe)
¼ oz. Banana Syrup (see recipe)
2 oz. unaged rum
Freshly grated nutmeg, for garnish

Place the Nacional Biz, juices, syrups, and rum in a cocktail shaker, fill it two-thirds of the way with ice, and shake until chilled.

Strain over large ice cubes into a rocks glass, garnish with the grated nutmeg, and enjoy.

Nacional Biz: Combine ¼ oz. banana liqueur, ¼ oz. Suze, and ¼ oz. apricot liqueur.

Yuzu Syrup: Place 2 oz. yuzu juice, 1 cup water, and 1 cup honey in a saucepan and bring to a boil over medium heat, stirring to combine. Remove the pan from heat and let the syrup cool completely before using or storing.

Banana Syrup: Place 2 peeled and sliced bananas and 1 cup sugar in a saucepan, stir until the bananas are coated, and let them macerate for 3 hours. Add ½ cup water and a pinch of fine sea salt and bring the mixture to a boil over medium heat, stirring to dissolve the sugar. Remove the pan from heat and let the syrup cool. Strain the syrup before using or storing in the refrigerator, where the syrup will keep for up to 1 month.

THE TOUGH GET GOING

THE TOUGH GET GOING

1½ oz. Royal Standard Dry Rum
½ oz. fresh orange juice
½ oz. Orgeat (see page 103)
½ oz. curaçao
¼ oz. fresh lime juice
½ oz. Santa Teresa 1796 Rum
1 strip of orange peel, for garnish

Place all of the ingredients, except for the Santa Teresa Rum and garnish, in a cocktail shaker, fill it two-thirds of the way with ice, and shake vigorously until chilled.

Fill a large tumbler with crushed ice and strain the cocktail over it.

Float the Santa Teresa Rum on top of the cocktail, pouring it slowly over the back of a spoon.

Garnish with the strip of orange peel and enjoy.

CAIPIRINHA

1 lime, cut into 8 wedges
2 brown sugar cubes
2 oz. cachaça

Place the lime wedges and sugar cubes in a highball glass and muddle.

Add crushed ice and top with the cachaça.

Stir until chilled and enjoy.

DAIQUIRI

At the tail end of the nineteenth century, Cuba was finally extricating itself from Spanish rule, but little could Cubans have known how their partnership with the United States would become of such geopolitical import over the course of the twentieth century. As soon as the peace treaty with Spain was signed, US exploratory expeditions were sent into the iron ore mines of the Sierra Maestra mountains, where there just so happens to be a town called Daiquirí. It was in this town that engineer Jennings Stockton Cox Jr. first saw the locals mixing Bacardí Carta Blanca with their coffee. Cox began toying around with various combinations before landing on rum, lime juice, and sugar. He and his cohorts took to drinking them in the morning, and one fine day they collectively decided to name the drink after the place where they first drank it.

2 oz. unaged rum

½ oz. fresh lime juice

1 teaspoon caster (superfine) sugar

1 lime wheel, for garnish

Chill a coupe in the freezer.

Place the rum, juice, and sugar in a cocktail shaker, fill it two-thirds of the way with ice, and shake until chilled.

Strain into the chilled coupe, garnish with the lime wheel, and enjoy.

SEA BEAST

¾ oz. fresh lime juice

¾ oz. passion fruit puree

¾ oz. Fernet-Branca

1 oz. Demerara Syrup (see page 65)

1½ oz. rum

Place all of the ingredients in a cocktail shaker, fill it two-thirds of the way with ice, and shake until chilled.

Strain over ice into a highball glass and enjoy.

THE PROJECT

2 oz. aged rum

¼ oz. Cynar

1 oz. Aperol

¼ oz. Coffee Syrup (see recipe)

1 torched orange twist, for garnish

3 coffee beans, for garnish

Place the rum, Cynar, Aperol, and syrup in a cocktail shaker, fill it two-thirds of the way with ice, and shake until chilled.

Double strain over an ice sphere into a rocks glass, garnish with the torched orange twist and coffee beans, and enjoy.

Coffee Syrup: Place 1 cup water, 2¼ oz. brewed espresso, a dash of cinnamon, and a dash of chili powder in a saucepan and bring to a boil, stirring occasionally. Add 2 cups sugar and stir until it has dissolved. Remove the pan from heat and let the syrup cool. Strain before using or storing.

THE RUM DIARY

2 oz. Brugal 1888 Rum

½ oz. Amaro Nonino Quintessentia

½ oz. Aperol

2 dashes of Angostura bitters

1 strip of lemon peel, for garnish

Place the rum, amaro, Aperol, and bitters in a mixing glass, fill it two-thirds of the way with ice, and stir until chilled.

Strain into a coupe, garnish with the strip of lemon peel, and enjoy.

JEAN LAFITTE COCKTAIL

1 teaspoon caster (superfine) sugar

2 dashes of absinthe

2 dashes of curaçao

1½ oz. Haitian rum

1 egg yolk

Chill a coupe in the freezer.

Place the sugar, absinthe, and curaçao in a cocktail shaker and muddle.

Add the rum, egg yolk, and ice and shake until chilled.

Strain into the chilled coupe and enjoy.

PERFECT STORM

1 oz. Plantation O.F.T.D. rum

1 oz. Banks 5 Island Rum

¾ oz. pineapple juice

½ oz. fresh lime juice

½ oz. Rhubarb Syrup (see recipe)

½ oz. Honey & Ginger Syrup (see page 231)

½ oz. grenadine

Chocolate-Infused 151 (see recipe)

1 pineapple leaf, for garnish

1 Luxardo maraschino cherry, for garnish

Fill a mixing glass with crushed ice and add all of the ingredients, except for the infused rum and garnishes. Use the swizzle method (see page 9) to combine.

Fill a Collins glass with pebble ice and strain the cocktail over it.

Float the infused rum on top of the cocktail, pouring it slowly over the back of the spoon.

Garnish the cocktail with the pineapple leaf and maraschino cherry and enjoy.

Rhubarb Syrup: Place 1 cup rhubarb puree, 2 cups sugar, 2 cups water, and the zest of ½ lemon in a saucepan and bring to a boil, stirring to dissolve the sugar. Remove the pan from heat and let the syrup cool completely. Strain before using or storing.

Chocolate-Infused 151: Place 2 cups dark chocolate chips and a 750 ml bottle of 151-proof rum in a large mason jar and let the mixture steep at room temperature for 24 hours. Strain before using or storing.

THE ARMANDE

2 dashes of Bittermens Xocolatl Mole Bitters

2 teaspoons crème de cacao

1 oz. Jamaican rum

1 oz. bourbon

Salt, to taste

Fill a rocks glass with ice and add all of the ingredients.

Stir until chilled and enjoy.

TROPIC PUNCH

2 oz. aged rum

½ oz. Aperol

1 oz. pineapple juice

1 oz. orange juice

½ oz. fresh lime juice

½ oz. agave nectar

Dash of egg white

Freshly grated nutmeg, for garnish

1 orange wheel, for garnish

Place the rum, Aperol, juices, agave nectar, and egg white in a cocktail shaker, fill it two-thirds of the way with ice, and shake until chilled.

Strain over ice into a highball glass, garnish with the grated nutmeg and orange wheel, and enjoy.

KAMA'AINA

½ oz. #9 (see recipe)

1 oz. spiced rum

1 oz. rhum agricole

1 oz. guava nectar

½ oz. cream of coconut

½ oz. fresh lime juice

2 dashes of Angostura bitters

1 edible orchid blossom, for garnish

Place the #9, rum, rhum agricole, guava nectar, cream of coconut, and lime juice in a cocktail shaker, fill it two-thirds of the way with crushed ice, and shake until chilled.

Pour the contents of the shaker into a tiki glass and top with the bitters.

Garnish with the orchid blossom and enjoy.

#9: Combine 2 oz. Ginger Syrup (see page 97) with 1 oz. almond paste. Add 1 teaspoon St. Elizabeth Allspice Dram or Alamea Pimento Liqueur and stir to combine. Use as desired.

IF YOU LIKE PIÑA COLADAS

2 oz. preferred rum blend

2 oz. fresh pineapple juice

1 oz. cream of coconut

¼ oz. fresh lemon juice

3 coffee beans

½ oz. Lustau Pedro Ximénéz Sherry

1 Luxardo maraschino cherry, for garnish

Fresh mint, for garnish

Fill a Hurricane glass with crushed ice.

Build the cocktail in the glass, adding all of the ingredients, except for the sherry and garnishes, to the glass in the order that they are listed.

Float the sherry on top of the cocktail, pouring it slowly over the back of a spoon.

Garnish the cocktail with the maraschino cherry and fresh mint and enjoy.

NEW ORLEANS PRESIDENTE

½ oz. grenadine

1½ oz. rum

½ oz. orange juice

Place all of the ingredients in a cocktail shaker, fill it two-thirds of the way with ice, and shake until chilled.

Strain into a cocktail glass and enjoy.

IF YOU LIKE PIÑA COLADAS

WINES, LIQUEURS & OTHER SPIRITS

Throughout the history of making cocktails, liqueurs were little more than sidekicks, supporting players, there to help the principals look their best. They were invaluable, essential, but seen as not being versatile or deep enough to carry the weight for an entire cocktail. They were one-note, capable of being additive, but incapable of occupying a prominent place. But, as with a Neil Young guitar solo or Mariano Rivera's cutter, sometimes we discover that a pony with one trick, if it is deployed expertly, proves to be irresistible. There is something appealing about a cocktail that boldly leads with the effortless complexity of an amaro, the spicy, bitter citrus of Campari, or the vegetal, herbaceous, and tobacco flavors present in Green Chartreuse, a fearlessness that appeals to our minds and tests the tastebuds in unexpected and delightful ways.

One benefit of a drink built around liqueurs and other off-the-well-worn-path spirits is that they cause us to pause where we would otherwise breeze past, cause us to take a moment and appreciate some aspect that had always been hidden away, crowded out by some other element. In a way, they allow us to love what we love in a deeper, fuller manner. So, whatever your favorite occupant of the "second tier" is, start thinking about ways to elevate it to the fore, and celebrate it in full.

NAKED & FAMOUS

¾ oz. Yellow Chartreuse

¾ oz. mezcal

¾ oz. Aperol

¾ oz. fresh lime juice

Chill a coupe in the freezer.

Place all of the ingredients in a cocktail shaker, fill it two-thirds of the way with ice, and shake until chilled.

Strain into the chilled coupe and enjoy.

DRINK OF LAUGHTER & FORGETTING

1½ oz. Cynar

½ oz. Green Chartreuse

¾ oz. fresh lime juice

½ oz. Demerara Syrup (see page 65)

14 drops of Angostura bitters, for garnish

Place all of the ingredients, except for the garnish, in a cocktail shaker, fill it two-thirds of the way with ice, and shake until chilled.

Strain into the cocktail glass, garnish with the bitters, and enjoy.

KIR ST. LOUIS

½ oz. St-Germain

1 oz. Giffard Crème de Pamplemousse Rose

Champagne, to top

1 grapefruit twist, for garnish

Place the St-Germain and liqueur in a Champagne flute.

Top with Champagne, garnish with the grapefruit twist, and enjoy.

SIDECAR

Sugar, for the rim

1½ oz. Cognac

¾ oz. Cointreau

¾ oz. fresh lemon juice

1 lemon twist, for garnish

Wet the rim of a coupe and rim it with sugar.

Place the Cognac, Cointreau, and lemon juice in a cocktail shaker, fill it two-thirds of the way with ice, and shake until chilled.

Strain into the rimmed coupe, garnish with the lemon twist, and enjoy.

PERSEPHONE

1 oz. applejack

½ oz. fresh lemon juice

½ oz. Simple Syrup (see page 16)

½ oz. sloe gin

¾ oz. dry vermouth

Chill a coupe in the freezer.

Place all of the ingredients in a mixing glass, fill it two-thirds of the way with ice, and stir until chilled.

Strain into the chilled coupe and enjoy.

CHARTREUSE SLUSHY

CHARTREUSE SLUSHY

2¼ oz. tart lemonade

1 oz. Green Chartreuse

2½ oz. Demerara Syrup (see page 65)

Place all of the ingredients in a blender, add 4 oz. crushed ice, and puree until smooth.

Pour the drink into a snifter and enjoy.

ALABAMA SLAMMER

¾ oz. peach liqueur

¾ oz. amaretto

¾ oz. sloe gin

¾ oz. vodka

6 oz. orange juice

Dash of grenadine

1 orange slice, for garnish

1 maraschino cherry, for garnish

Fill a Collins glass with ice, add the liqueur, amaretto, gin, and vodka, and stir until chilled.

Top with the orange juice and grenadine, garnish with the orange slice and maraschino cherry, and enjoy.

SNOWBALL

2 oz. advocaat

Dash of fresh lime juice

Dash of maple syrup

Lemonade, to top

Dollop of whipped cream, for garnish

1 maraschino cherry, for garnish

Place the advocaat, lime juice, and maple syrup in a cocktail shaker, fill it two-thirds of the way with ice, and shake until chilled.

Strain into a mason jar and top with lemonade.

Garnish with the whipped cream and maraschino cherry and enjoy.

PIMM'S CUP

1 oz. Pimm's No. 1

2 oz. lemon-lime soda

½ oz. Luxardo maraschino liqueur

2 cucumber wheels, for garnish

1 lemon wheel, for garnish

Fill a highball glass with ice, add the Pimm's No. 1, soda, and Luxardo, and stir until chilled.

Garnish with the cucumber wheels and lemon wheel and enjoy.

CERISE SOIR

1 teaspoon Simple Syrup (see page 16)
Dash of fresh lemon juice
1 teaspoon syrup from a jar of Griottines
1 oz. Rhum Clément Créole Shrubb
2 Griottines, for garnish

Chill a Nick & Nora glass in the freezer.

Place the Simple Syrup, lemon juice, Griottines syrup, and Rhum Clément Créole Shrubb in a cocktail shaker, fill it two-thirds of the way with ice, and shake until chilled.

Strain into the chilled Nick & Nora glass, garnish with the Griottines, and enjoy.

BARON OF BROOKLYN

Dash of Bittermens Xocolatl Mole Bitters
Dash of Angostura bitters
½ oz. Suze
½ oz. Giffard Banane du Brésil liqueur
1½ oz. port
1½ oz. cachaça
1 long lemon twist, for garnish

Place the bitters, Suze, liqueur, port, and cachaça in a mixing glass, fill it two-thirds of the way with ice, and stir until chilled.

Strain over a large ice cube into a snifter, garnish with the long lemon twist, and enjoy.

CORPSE REVIVER

Juice of ¼ lemon

2 oz. Pernod

Champagne, to top

Place a large ice cube in a cocktail glass, add the lemon juice and Pernod, and stir until chilled.

Top with Champagne and enjoy.

FLIRTBIRD

Li hing mui plum powder, for the rim

1½ oz. shochu

1 oz. yuzu juice

½ oz. agave nectar

1 fresh shiso leaf, torn, plus 1 for garnish

Wet the rim of a rocks glass and rim it with plum powder.

Place the shochu, yuzu juice, agave nectar, and torn shiso leaf in a cocktail shaker, fill it two-thirds of the way with ice, and shake until chilled.

Strain over a large ice cube into the rimmed glass, garnish with an additional fresh shiso leaf, and enjoy.

DISAPPEARING ACT

1 oz. Lillet

½ oz. aquavit

½ oz. fresh lemon juice

½ oz. Simple Syrup (see page 16)

1 teaspoon Giffard Crème de Pêche de Vigne

Sparkling wine, to top

1 lemon twist, for garnish

Place the Lillet, aquavit, lemon juice, syrup, and liqueur in a cocktail shaker, fill it two-thirds of the way with ice, and shake until chilled.

Strain into a coupe and top with sparkling wine.

Garnish with the lemon twist and enjoy.

MR. OCTOBER

1½ oz. applejack

¾ oz. Cinnamon Syrup (see page 262)

¾ oz. fresh lemon juice

½ oz. Galliano

2 dashes of St. Elizabeth Allspice Dram

Freshly grated nutmeg, for garnish

Chill a coupe in the freezer.

Place the applejack, syrup, lemon juice, Galliano, and allspice dram in a cocktail shaker, fill it two-thirds of the way with ice, and shake until chilled.

Double strain into the chilled coupe, garnish with grated nutmeg, and enjoy.

MACE

THE LAST WORD

½ oz. Green Chartreuse

½ oz. Luxardo maraschino liqueur

½ oz. gin

½ oz. fresh lime juice

1 lime twist, for garnish

Chill a coupe in the freezer.

Place the Chartreuse, Luxardo, gin, and lime juice in a cocktail shaker, fill it two-thirds of the way with ice, and shake until chilled.

Strain into the chilled coupe, garnish with the lime twist, and enjoy.

MACE

1 oz. aquavit

1 oz. Aperol

½ oz. fresh orange juice

½ oz. freshly pressed beet juice

¾ oz. syrup from a can of Lucia Young Coconut

Mace tincture, to spritz

Place all of the ingredients, except for the tincture, in a cocktail shaker, fill it two-thirds of the way with ice, and shake until chilled.

Double strain into a coupe, spritz the cocktail with mace tincture, and enjoy.

ROME WITH A VIEW

1 oz. Campari
1 oz. dry vermouth
½ oz. fresh lime juice
¼ oz. Simple Syrup (see page 16)
Club soda, to top
1 orange wheel, for garnish
1 lime twist, for garnish

Place the Campari, vermouth, lime juice, and syrup in a cocktail shaker, fill it two-thirds of the way with ice, and shake until chilled.

Strain over ice into a Collins glass and top with club soda.

Garnish with the orange wheel and lime twist and enjoy.

GARIBALDI

1½ oz. Campari
Fresh orange juice, to top
1 orange wedge, for garnish

Place 2 ice cubes in a Collins glass, add the Campari and a splash of orange juice, and stir until chilled.

Add 1 more ice cube and top with orange juice.

Garnish with the orange wedge and enjoy.

CAMPARI COLADA

3 oz. fresh pineapple juice

1 oz. cream of coconut

1 oz. heavy cream

2 oz. Campari

1 orange slice, for garnish

1 Luxardo maraschino cherry, for garnish

Place the juice, cream of coconut, heavy cream, and Campari in a cocktail shaker and dry shake for 10 to 15 seconds.

Pour over crushed ice into a tall tiki mug and use the swizzle method (see page 9) to chill the cocktail.

Garnish with the orange slice and maraschino cherry and enjoy.

ABSINTHE FRAPPE

1½ oz. absinthe

¼ oz. Simple Syrup (see page 16)

2 oz. club soda

Fresh mint, for garnish

Place the absinthe, syrup, and club soda in a cocktail shaker, fill it two-thirds of the way with ice, and shake until chilled.

Strain over crushed ice into a Julep cup, garnish with fresh mint, and enjoy.

SINGANI FIZZ

1½ oz. Saffron-Infused Singani (see recipe)
1 oz. Vanilla Syrup (see page 52)
1 oz. fresh lemon juice
1 oz. heavy cream
3 dashes of cardamom bitters
1 egg white
Splash of club soda
2 fresh shiso leaves, for garnish

Place all of the ingredients, except for the club soda and garnish, in a cocktail shaker and dry shake for 10 seconds.

Add ice and shake until chilled. Let the cocktail rest for 30 seconds.

Strain over ice into a Collins glass and top with the club soda.

Garnish with the shiso leaves and enjoy.

Saffron-Infused Singani: Place 2 pinches of saffron threads and a 750 ml bottle of Singani 63 in a large mason jar and let the mixture steep overnight. Strain before using or storing.

AMERICANO

1 oz. Campari
1 oz. sweet vermouth
1 oz. club soda
1 lemon slice, for garnish

Fill a rocks glass with ice, add the Campari and sweet vermouth, and stir until chilled.

Top with the club soda, garnish with the lemon slice, and enjoy.

SINGANI FIZZ

MAGIC TREE

2 slices of cucumber

1½ oz. Stoupakis Homeric Chios Mastiha Spirit

½ oz. Suze

½ oz. navy-strength gin (Royal Dock preferred)

¾ oz. fresh lime juice

¼ oz. Simple Syrup (see page 16)

7 drops of The Bitter Truth Cucumber Bitters, for garnish

Place the cucumber in a cocktail shaker and muddle.

Add ice and all of the remaining ingredients, except for the garnish, and shake until chilled.

Double strain the cocktail into a coupe, garnish with the bitters, and enjoy.

GREEN GODDESS PUNCH

½ oz. absinthe

1 oz. fresh lime juice

1 oz. Simple Syrup (see page 16)

4 oz. Topo Chico

Fresh mint, for garnish

Fill a Collins glass with ice, add the absinthe, lime juice, and syrup, and stir until chilled.

Top with the Topo Chico, garnish with fresh mint, and enjoy.

GRASSHOPPER

1 oz. green crème de menthe

1 oz. white crème de cacao

1 oz. heavy cream

Chill a cocktail glass in the freezer.

Place all of the ingredients in a cocktail shaker, fill it two-thirds of the way with ice, and shake until chilled.

Strain into the chilled cocktail glass and enjoy.

THE VELLOCET

2 oz. Green Chartreuse

1¼ oz. pineapple juice

¾ oz. fresh lime juice

½ oz. Velvet Falernum

2 dashes of Angostura bitters

2 dashes of Peychaud's bitters

Fresh mint, for garnish

Fill a Collins glass with crushed ice, add the Chartreuse, juices, falernum, and bitters, and use the swizzle method (see page 9) to combine.

Garnish with fresh mint and enjoy.

ONE OF THESE NIGHTS

1¼ oz. Amaro Lucano

¾ oz. Cognac

¼ oz. Pierre Ferrand Dry Curaçao

¼ oz. fresh lemon juice

½ oz. Orgeat (see page 103)

¾ oz. cold-brew coffee

Dash of Peychaud's bitters

1 torched star anise pod, for garnish

Place the amaro, Cognac, curaçao, lemon juice, Orgeat, coffee, and bitters in a cocktail shaker, fill it two-thirds of the way with ice, and shake until chilled.

Double strain into a coupe, garnish with the torched star anise, and enjoy.

GINGER SHANDY

Handful of fresh mint

4 oz. wheat beer

12 oz. ginger beer

1 lemon slice, for garnish

Rub the mint along the rim of a mason jar or pint glass, tear them in half, and place them in the jar or glass.

Add ice, the wheat beer and ginger beer, and stir until chilled.

Garnish with the lemon slice and enjoy.

BLACK VELVET

4 oz. Champagne
Splash of sparkling cider
4 oz. stout

Place the Champagne and sparkling cider in a pint glass.

Top with the stout, pouring it slowly over the back of a spoon, and enjoy.

IPA OVER ICE

3 oz. grapefruit juice
1 oz. Campari
Dash of Simple Syrup (see page 16)
8 oz. IPA
1 orange wedge, for garnish

Place the juice, Campari, and syrup in a cocktail shaker, fill it two-thirds of the way with ice, and shake until chilled.

Strain over ice into a pint glass and top with the IPA.

Garnish with the orange wedge and enjoy.

DOVER CLUB

4 raspberries, plus 2 for garnish
½ oz. Simple Syrup (see page 16)
3 oz. Pinot Noir
1½ oz. orange juice
1 teaspoon raspberry preserves
1 egg white

Place the raspberries and syrup in a cocktail shaker and muddle.

Add the Pinot Noir, orange juice, raspberry preserves, and egg white and dry shake for 15 seconds.

Add ice and shake until chilled.

Strain into a wineglass, garnish with the additional raspberries, and enjoy.

DE WALLEN

1 strawberry, plus 1 for garnish
¾ oz. grenadine
1½ oz. Pedro Ximénez sherry
1½ oz. Muscat
Champagne, to top
1 Griottine, for garnish

Place the strawberry and grenadine in a cocktail shaker and muddle.

Add ice, the sherry and Muscat, and shake until chilled.

Strain into a small snifter and top with Champagne.

Garnish with the Griottine and additional strawberry and enjoy.

BELLINI

1 oz. peach nectar
Champagne, to top

Place the peach nectar in a Champagne flute, top with Champagne, and enjoy.

BUCK'S FIZZ

2 oz. Champagne
1 oz. orange juice

Place the Champagne in a Champagne flute, top with the orange juice, and enjoy.

LA VIE EN ROSE

1 oz. Strawberry & Gin Reduction (see recipe)
3 oz. red wine
Champagne, to top
2 to 3 strawberries, for garnish

Place the reduction and red wine in a wineglass and stir to combine.

Top with Champagne, garnish with the strawberries, and enjoy.

Strawberry & Gin Reduction: Place 2 oz. gin and 4 strawberries in a food processor and puree until smooth. Strain into a small saucepan through a fine sieve and cook over medium heat until the mixture has reduced by half. Let the reduction cool completely before using.

MONTEZUMA

1 oz. pisco
½ oz. Midori
1 oz. kiwi puree
1 oz. Sauvignon Blanc
¾ oz. Simple Syrup (see page 16)
1 lime wheel, for garnish

Place all of the ingredients, except for the garnish, in a cocktail shaker, fill it two-thirds of the way with ice, and shake until chilled.

Double strain into a coupe, garnish with the lime wheel, and enjoy.

CLASSIC WHITE SANGRIA

1 (750 ml) bottle of dry white wine
1 cup seedless green grapes, halved
½ cup seedless red grapes, halved
2 cups white grape juice
¼ cup brandy
2 cups seltzer water

Place the wine, grapes, grape juice, and brandy in a large pitcher, cover it, and chill in the refrigerator for at least 4 hours.

When ready to serve, add ice and the seltzer water.

Stir until chilled and enjoy.

MONTEZUMA

MIMOSA

1½ oz. orange juice

1½ oz. Champagne

1 orange slice, for garnish

Place the orange juice and Champagne in a Champagne flute, garnish with the orange slice, and enjoy.

BERRY SANGRIA

1 cup fresh strawberries, halved and juice reserved

1 cup fresh or frozen blueberries

⅔ cup fresh or frozen blackberries

⅓ cup brandy

2 (750 ml) bottles of dry red wine

2 cups strawberry seltzer water

Place the strawberries, strawberry juice, blueberries, blackberries, and brandy in a large pitcher and stir to combine.

Add the wine and stir to combine. Cover the pitcher and chill in the refrigerator for 4 hours.

When ready to serve, add ice and the seltzer.

Stir until chilled and enjoy.

CLASSIC RED WINE SANGRIA

1 (750 ml) bottle of dry red wine

2 oranges, sliced thin

2 Granny Smith apples, cored, seeded, and diced

¼ cup brandy

1 cup lemon seltzer water

Place the wine, oranges, apples, and brandy in a large pitcher, cover it, and chill in the refrigerator for at least 4 hours.

When ready to serve, add ice and the seltzer water.

Stir until chilled and enjoy.

PEACH SANGRIA

1 peach, pitted and diced

⅓ cup peach nectar

⅓ cup peach liqueur

2 (750 ml) bottles of dry white wine

6 cups peach seltzer water

Place the peach, peach nectar, and liqueur in a large pitcher and stir to combine.

Add the wine and stir to combine. Cover the pitcher and chill in the refrigerator for 4 hours.

When ready to serve, add ice and the seltzer.

Stir until chilled and enjoy.

GO AHEAD ROMEO

GO AHEAD ROMEO

6 Aperol Ice Cubes (see recipe)

4 oz. Prosecco

1 orange twist, for garnish

Place the Aperol Ice Cubes in a snifter and pour the Prosecco over them.

Garnish with the orange twist and enjoy.

Aperol Ice Cubes: Combine ¼ cup Aperol and ¾ cup water, pour the mixture into ice cube trays, and freeze until solid.

MOLOKAI MISHAP

1 oz. Cocchi Americano

1 oz. peach liqueur

1 oz. pineapple juice

1 oz. rhum agricole

8 drops of Bittermens 'Elemakule Tiki Bitters

Place large ice cubes in a double rocks glass and add all of the ingredients.

Stir until chilled and enjoy.

THE RIGHT SIDE OF JACKSON

2 oz. fino sherry

¾ oz. Grand Marnier

Place the sherry and Grand Marnier in a mixing glass, fill it two-thirds of the way with ice, and gently stir until chilled.

Strain into a snifter and enjoy.

RARE STAMPS

1½ oz. Cocchi Americano

1 oz. aged rum

½ oz. Cardamaro

1 lemon twist, for garnish

Place the Cocchi Americano, rum, and Cardamaro in a mixing glass, fill it two-thirds of the way with ice, and stir until chilled.

Strain into a coupe, garnish with the lemon twist, and enjoy.

SUNDAY MORNING COMING DOWN

3 to 4 fresh mint leaves, plus more for garnish

1½ oz. Madeira

1 oz. rum

¼ oz. Demerara Syrup (see page 65)

Place the fresh mint in a Julep cup and gently muddle.

Add crushed ice, the Madeira, rum, and syrup, and stir until chilled.

Top with more crushed ice, garnish with additional fresh mint, and enjoy.

SAKURA MARTINI

2½ oz. dry sake

1 oz. gin

¼ teaspoon Luxardo maraschino liqueur

1 edible cherry blossom, for garnish

Place the sake, gin, and Luxardo in a mixing glass, fill it two-thirds of the way with ice, and stir until chilled.

Strain into a cocktail glass, garnish with the cherry blossom, and enjoy.

LIPSTICK & ROUGE

¾ oz. Aperol

¾ oz. Luxardo Amaretto di Saschira

¾ oz. fresh lemon juice

3 oz. Prosecco

1 lemon twist, for garnish

Place the Aperol, Luxardo, and lemon juice in a cocktail shaker, fill it two-thirds of the way with ice, and shake until chilled.

Strain into a Champagne flute and top with the Prosecco.

Garnish with the lemon twist and enjoy.

THE LITTLEJOHN COBBLER

1½ oz. Kumquat & Strawberry Cordial (see recipe)

¾ oz. Pedro Ximénez sherry

¾ oz. oloroso sherry

¾ oz. Plantation O.F.T.D. rum

¼ oz. fresh lime juice

Fresh mint, for garnish

1 strawberry slice, for garnish

1 kumquat slice, for garnish

Dusting of confectioners' sugar, for garnish

Place the cordial, sherries, rum, and lime juice in a cocktail shaker, fill it two-thirds of the way with ice, and shake until chilled.

Strain over ice into a Julep cup, garnish with fresh mint, the strawberry slice, kumquat slice, and confectioners' sugar, and enjoy.

Kumquat & Strawberry Cordial: Combine 3 cups sliced strawberries and 3 tablespoons sugar in a bowl and let the mixture sit for 1 hour, mashing occasionally so that the strawberries release all of their juice. Stir in 1 cup kumquat juice and ¾ cup vodka and strain before using or storing.

THREE EMMAS COCKTAIL

1 oz. Beer & Rose Cordial (see recipe)
1 oz. amontillado sherry
¾ oz. The Botanist Gin
½ oz. fresh lemon juice
½ oz. grapefruit juice
2 fresh basil leaves, for garnish

Place the cordial, sherry, gin, and juices in a cocktail shaker, fill it two-thirds of the way with ice, and shake until chilled.

Strain over crushed ice into a Nick & Nora glass, garnish with the fresh basil, and enjoy.

Beer & Rose Cordial: Combine 2 (12 oz.) bottles of lager and 3 cups sugar in a medium saucepan and warm over low heat. Stir until the sugar has dissolved, making sure the mixture does not come to a boil. Remove the pan from heat and let the mixture cool completely. Stir in a 8½ oz. bottle of The East India Company Rose Cordial and ½ oz. rose water and store in the refrigerator.

BANANA PUNCH

1½ oz. apricot brandy
1 oz. vodka
½ oz. fresh lime juice
Club soda, to top
½ banana, sliced, for garnish
Fresh mint, for garnish

Fill a Collins glass with crushed ice, add the brandy, vodka, and lime juice, and top with club soda.

Stir until chilled, garnish with the banana slices and fresh mint, and enjoy.

DECI'S ROOMMATE

1 oz. calvados
¾ oz. fresh lime juice
½ oz. Demerara Syrup (see page 65)
2 oz. sparkling rosé
Fresh mint, for garnish

Place the calvados, lime juice, and syrup in a cocktail shaker, fill it two-thirds of the way with ice, and shake until chilled.

Add the sparking rosé to the shaker and strain over ice into a rocks glass.

Garnish with fresh mint and enjoy.

HIBISCUS TEA COBBLER

1 teaspoon grenadine
1 lemon wheel, sliced in half
1 oz. curaçao
1 oz. Cognac
1½ oz. iced hibiscus tea
1 lemon wheel, for garnish
Dehydrated hibiscus blossoms, for garnish
1 Luxardo maraschino cherry, for garnish

Place the grenadine and lemon wheel in a Collins glass and muddle.

Add the remaining ingredients, except for the garnishes, and then fill the glass with crushed ice.

Stir until the cocktail is chilled and combined.

Top the cocktail with more crushed ice, garnish with the lemon wheel, dehydrated hibiscus blossoms, and maraschino cherry, and enjoy.

VELVET CLUB

1 oz. Cognac

½ oz. Lillet

½ oz. crème de cacao

Champagne, to top

Place the Cognac, Lillet, and crème de cacao in a mixing glass, fill it two-thirds of the way with ice, and stir until chilled.

Strain into a coupe, top with Champagne, and enjoy.

PERUVIAN SHRUB

1 oz. Red Fruits Shrub (see recipe)

1¾ oz. pisco

½ oz. fresh apple juice

2 teaspoons Cherry Heering

Dash of rhubarb bitters

½ oz. Corona

1 blackberry, for garnish

1 sprig of fresh thyme, for garnish

Place the shrub, pisco, juice, liqueur, bitters, and Corona in a cocktail shaker and fill it two-thirds of the way with ice.

Pour the drink back and forth between the cocktail shaker and a mixing glass until chilled.

Strain into a rocks glass, garnish with the blackberry and fresh thyme, and enjoy.

Red Fruits Shrub: Combine ½ cup sugar, ½ cup white wine vinegar, ¼ cup sliced strawberries, and ¼ cup raspberries in a small saucepan and simmer over medium heat until the berries release their juices. Strain the shrub into a jar and chill in the refrigerator for 3 days before using.

APRICOT FUZZ

2 oz. apricot brandy

1 oz. fresh lemon juice

½ oz. fresh lime juice

1 teaspoon Simple Syrup (see page 16)

Club soda, to top

Place the brandy, juices, and syrup in a cocktail shaker, fill it two-thirds of the way with ice, and shake until chilled.

Strain over ice into a highball glass and top with club soda.

Gently stir to combine and enjoy.

PULP FICTION

2 oz. Cognac

1 oz. apple liqueur

2 oz. apple juice

Lemonade, to top

1 apple slice, for garnish

Place the Cognac, liqueur, and apple juice in a cocktail shaker, fill it two-thirds of the way with ice, and shake until chilled.

Strain over ice into a highball glass and top with lemonade.

Garnish with the apple slice and enjoy.

CARRIED AWAY

1½ oz. aquavit
¾ oz. Rhum Clément Mahina Coco coconut liqueur
½ oz. fresh lemon juice
¼ oz. Honey Syrup (see page 64)
2 lime wheels, for garnish
Freshly grated cinnamon, for garnish

Place all of the ingredients, except for the garnishes, in a cocktail shaker, fill it two-thirds of the way with ice, and shake until chilled.

Strain over ice into a snifter, garnish with the lime wheels and cinnamon, and enjoy.

SAKE NIGHT IN CANADA

2 oz. sake
½ oz. Singani 63
¼ oz. Pierre Ferrand Dry Curaçao
1 oz. aquafaba
¾ oz. grapefruit juice
¼ oz. Demerara Syrup (see page 65)
2 to 3 dashes of Scrappy's Lime Bitters, for garnish

Place all of the ingredients, except for the garnish, in a cocktail shaker, fill it two-thirds of the way with ice, and shake until chilled.

Strain over ice into a rocks glass, garnish with the bitters, and enjoy.

B & B

1 oz. Bénédictine
1 oz. brandy

Fill a rocks glass with ice, add all of the ingredients, stir until chilled, and enjoy.

CARRIED AWAY

MOLE YETI

1 oz. añejo tequila

¾ oz. Leopold Bros. Three Pins Alpine Herbal Liqueur

½ teaspoon chipotle chile powder

6 oz. chocolate stout

Place the tequila and liqueur in a mixing glass, fill it two-thirds of the way with ice, and stir until chilled.

Strain into a clean mixing glass, add the chipotle chile powder, and stir vigorously to completely incorporate it.

Strain into a goblet, slowly pour in the stout, and enjoy.

MORNING GLORY

1 oz. rye whiskey

1 oz. Cognac

1 teaspoon Simple Syrup (see page 16)

½ teaspoon Grand Marnier

2 dashes of Angostura bitters

Dash of absinthe

1 oz. club soda

1 strip of lemon peel, for garnish

Chill a cocktail glass in the freezer.

Place the rye, Cognac, syrup, Grand Marnier, bitters, and absinthe in a mixing glass, fill it two-thirds of the way with ice, and stir until chilled.

Strain into the chilled cocktail glass and top with the club soda.

Express the strip of lemon peel over the drink, garnish the cocktail with it, and enjoy.

LE METRO

2 oz. Cognac
1 oz. crème de cassis
½ oz. fresh lemon juice
3 dashes of Peychaud's bitters
2 Griottines, for garnish

Chill a cocktail glass in the freezer.

Place the Cognac, crème de cassis, lemon juice, and bitters in a cocktail shaker, fill it two-thirds of the way with ice, and shake until chilled.

Strain into the chilled cocktail glass, garnish with the Griottines, and enjoy.

NEW JACK CITY

1¼ oz. umeshu
¾ oz. rye whiskey
¾ oz. applejack
4 teaspoons sweet vermouth
1 ginkgo leaf, for garnish

Place the umeshu, rye whiskey, applejack, and sweet vermouth in a mixing glass, fill it two-thirds of the way with ice, and stir until chilled.

Strain into a coupe or cocktail glass, garnish with the ginkgo leaf, and enjoy.

REJECT IN THE ATTIC

1 oz. Jägermeister

1 oz. Amaro Lucano

¾ oz. Cocchi Americano

¼ oz. Clear Creek Loganberry Liqueur

Q Sparkling Grapefruit soda, to top

Fill a Collins glass with ice and build the cocktail in the glass, adding the ingredients in the order they are listed.

Gently stir and enjoy.

BRANDY ALEXANDER

½ oz. brandy

½ oz. crème de cacao

½ oz. heavy cream

Chill a cocktail glass in the freezer.

Place all of the ingredients in a cocktail shaker, fill it two-thirds of the way with ice, and shake until chilled.

Strain into the chilled cocktail glass and enjoy.

OLD HICKORY

1½ oz. dry vermouth

1½ oz. sweet vermouth

2 dashes of Peychaud's bitters

Dash of orange bitters

1 lemon twist, for garnish

Fill a rocks glass with ice, add the vermouths and bitters, and stir until chilled.

Garnish with the lemon twist and enjoy.

BRANDY MILK PUNCH

3 oz. whole milk

1 oz. half-and-half

2 oz. brandy

1 oz. Simple Syrup (see page 16)

½ teaspoon pure vanilla extract

Freshly grated nutmeg, for garnish

Chill a rocks glass in the freezer.

Place the whole milk, half-and-half, brandy, syrup, and vanilla extract in a cocktail shaker, fill it two-thirds of the way with ice, and shake until chilled.

Strain into the chilled rocks glass, garnish with grated nutmeg, and enjoy.

CHAMPS-ÉLYSÉES

2 oz. Cognac

¾ oz. fresh lemon juice

¼ oz. Green Chartreuse

¼ oz. Simple Syrup (see page 16)

2 dashes of Angostura bitters

1 lemon twist, for garnish

Place all of the ingredients, except for the garnish, in a cocktail shaker, fill it two-thirds of the way with ice, and shake until chilled.

Double strain into a coupe, garnish with the lemon twist, and enjoy.

METRIC CONVERSIONS

WEIGHTS

1 oz. = 28 grams
2 oz. = 57 grams
4 oz. (¼ lb.) = 113 grams
8 oz. (½ lb.) = 227 grams
16 oz. (1 lb.) = 454 grams

VOLUME MEASURES

⅛ teaspoon = 0.6 ml
¼ teaspoon = 1.23 ml
½ teaspoon = 2.5 ml
1 teaspoon = 5 ml
1 tablespoon (3 teaspoons) = ½ fluid oz. = 15 ml
2 tablespoons = 1 fluid oz. = 29.5 ml
¼ cup (4 tablespoons) = 2 fluid oz. = 59 ml
⅓ cup (5⅓ tablespoons) = 2.7 fluid oz. = 80 ml
½ cup (8 tablespoons) = 4 fluid oz. = 120 ml
⅔ cup (10⅔ tablespoons) = 5.4 fluid oz. = 160 ml
¾ cup (12 tablespoons) = 6 fluid oz. = 180 ml
1 cup (16 tablespoons) = 8 fluid oz. = 240 ml

TEMPERATURE EQUIVALENTS

°F	°C	Gas Mark
225	110	¼
250	130	½
275	140	1
300	150	2
325	170	3
350	180	4
375	190	5
400	200	6
425	220	7
450	230	8
475	240	9
500	250	10

LENGTH MEASURES

1⁄16 inch = 1.6 mm
⅛ inch = 3 mm
¼ inch = 6.35 mm
½ inch = 1.25 cm
¾ inch = 2 cm
1 inch = 2.5 cm

INDEX

D